Journal of the Fictive Life

Howard Nemerov
Journal
of the
Fictive Life

With a new Preface

The University of Chicago Press

Chicago and London

The University of Chicago Press, Chicago 60637
The University of Chicago Press, Ltd., London

87 86 85 84 83 82 81   1 2 3 4 5

Library of Congress Cataloging in Publication Data
Nemerov, Howard.
    Journal of the fictive life.

    1. Nemerov, Howard—Diaries. 2. Authors,
American—20th century—Biography. I. Title.
PS3527.E5Z47 1981   818' .5403 [B]   81-10449
ISBN 0-226-57261-7 (pbk.)   AACR2

PREFACE TO THE PHOENIX EDITION

Reading over what I wrote in the summer of 1963 occasions some odd reflexions, and about time. The not-quite-young man who wrote it, where has he gone? Alexander, the son whose birth is recorded in its last sentence—he didn't yet have a name—and who will be eighteen on the eighteenth anniversary of its completion, gave to the news of its re-issue his term of highest approbation: "Kick-ass, Howard," though not without a small debate about whether the term should be two words, one word, or hyphenated, something dictionaries are not likely to tell us about for some time if ever (decision by his younger brother Jeremy, with family agreement). So there is one of the mysteries: time, growth, decline, whose nature is so strange that our ideas about it remain as primitive as they have been through, well, through time. Probably Augustine's account, in the XIth book of the *Confessions*, is still as good as we have, if subject to a couple of quibbles among physicists. Time is either a straight line, or a circle, or (in some rather alembicated views such as Spengler's or Yeats's) a spiral. We should be able to do better than those, but we don't.

A second mystery: the book's mode of working is admittedly, even avowedly, conditioned by the work of Sigmund Freud, *der goldene Sigi* as a friend called him, even if the author's exploration of the psychoanalytical way brought him out at last to the view of it as a plausible fraud. (But then, as Joyce says, He was jung and easily freudened.) He remembers, even if only as a screen memory, but a screen for what? Walking into a friend's house at age 14, swinging a copy of the Modern Library *Basic Writings of Sigmund Freud*, and being told by the friend's mother: "Don't read stuff like that, it'll make you sick." And so maybe it did.

Preface

The better part of two decades after the book, I look with respect if not total agreement at Sir Peter Medawar's observation: "Considered in its entirety, psychoanalysis won't do. It is an end product, moreover, like a dinosaur or a zeppelin; no better theory can ever be erected on its ruins, which will remain for ever one of the saddest and strangest of all landmarks in the history of twentieth century thought" (P. B. Medawar, *The Hope of Progress*, London, 1972). Well, I think, zeppelins might be about to come back, given new technology, and dinosaurs outlasted us exponentially. But the point is taken, only to yield to another: the immense power of idea and words, which brought some thoughts from one brain, beginning about 1900, to such a pitch of certainty and universality that they must have comforted manufacturers of couches mightily for better than half a century. Other instances will occur to my readers. But happily for myself I had always read Freud as an epic poet in spite of all his claims to science and its rigors: an epic poet who showed the tribe that its dreams made sense . . . sort of, and presented a technique for trying it out.

The third mystery I get from looking back on my book—but is it any longer 'my' book?—is the part of what we continue to call 'mind' in all this. You will remember the scholastic saying 'Nihil in intellectu quod non prius in sensus'? and Leibniz's cute addition, 'praeter intellectus ipse'? Well, I was able to phrase this in my own way, as a dialogue:
    —Don't worry, it's all in the mind.
    —Except the mind, which is in the body. Worry all you
      want.
Dear Reader, Dear Me (as I call you in the book, if you read that far), I hope this crude imitation of your own struggles may sometimes win your sympathy.

BOOK ONE

Reflexions of the Novelist Felix Ledger—A

Not knowing where to begin, that was the beginning; it might become the end, as well, the end before the beginning, the end that should formally exclude beginning. Pascal had said it: The last thing you get to know is what should come first.

Felix would rather not be found dead in possession of the remark, The Novel Is Dead. But he knew of a good many novels that showed how rumors of that sort get started.

One thing 'the novel' did, quietly, offhandedly, maybe by accident: It gave readers the possibility of believing in the past, in their own past, as substantially existing behind them (even though examination would have proved their memory of this past projected by means of novelistic fictions, hence absurdly at variance with what happened).

'The novel,' then, was a way of constructing a certain feeling of reality, rather than a reality, by means of formal presuppositions about life, especially the one which claimed that life was a story (with all the following propositions about purpose, identity, history, God). This idea the novel inherited rather casually from drama, from magical poetizing.

But the special technique which 'the novel' added to the tradition was what one may broadly call realism, meaning by this word only one aspect of what is usually meant; that aspect is *detail*.

A. Life is like a story, life is a story.
B. Detail.

The question of the existence of 'the novel' could not come up while B was regarded, was able to be regarded, as the intensifying means to doing A. But as soon as the amount of detail began to be perceived as possibly unlimited, as possibly photographic in essence—and a photography, so to say, of all five senses, plus memory, imagination, and thought—the relation of A and B had to become one of antagonism. The crucial, or balancing, example of this process was *Ulysses*, with its equal (and opposite) allegiance to mythos and chaos.

For a while after *Ulysses*, people continued to write 'the ordinary novel'; in fact, they still do, with more and less taste, skill, vigor, and intelligence.

On the other side, the solutions of the *nouvelle vague* seem to be necessarily implied as the consequence of what happens in *Ulysses*; but that doesn't make these vague novels any easier (or more nearly possible) for me to read. (I gave in to the pun; the novels are just the reverse of vague—except maybe in their total effect.)

Reflexions—B

The only way out is the way through, just as you cannot escape death except by dying. Being unable to write, you must examine in writing this being unable, which becomes for the present—henceforth?—the subject to which you are condemned.

The first thought is this: fear. I cannot write because I am afraid. Of what?

If I examine my sensations in the presence of 'an idea,' I get some hints of what the fear refers to.

What will other people say?

This is absurd, as well as being timid; but real life doesn't have the ideal character one learns to expect of it from novels, so it is necessary also to be absurd, timid, not ideal.

That is to say: A story, the germ of a design, comes from real life. From one's own more or less real life. Never mind how the imagination will transform it into something rich and strange and, above all, unrecognizable; that happens later, if at all. Meanwhile, the imagination has done nothing more than be somewhat entranced by what looks for a moment to be possible.

Soon after this being entranced, begins the fear of the opinion of others, which has a number of causes and expresses itself in several ways, all of which, however, have in common the object of making the writer give in, give up, give away.

Fear of writing about others. Several stories I should have wished to tell are set, to my mind, in untranslatably recognizable and peculiar circumstances, belong to particular individuals. It is enough to say: one's wife, one's colleagues, the situation of the place in which one lives for a long time.

Put down bluntly, the fear is seen to be somewhat silly; but it is necessary to add that if things disappeared just because they were seen to be silly this world would have a very different appearance. And yet it is perhaps not altogether silly: If I wrote about my wife photographically, so to say, it might well occasion me, as well as her, some domestic inconvenience.

But to do that would be bad art, and really to do it would be perhaps impossible anyhow. I wonder how much we could know of another person that would not turn out in the end to be a form of words, a formula thrown like a blanket over the sleeping form. So the fear begins to look silly again.

Or if I wrote about a college president, or two such, a college president and his successor, ought I not to fear displeasure, possible reprisals? Perhaps not. But yet this is one of the forms the fear takes, one of the ways in which, without being examined much in itself, it evokes resistances which disguise themselves as apathy, listlessness, loss of interest. . . .

It is remarkable, in fact, how much one's energies can be engaged in and stirred by an idea one day, and utterly unmoved, even bored, the next.

Or if I wrote about the circumstances of my father's illness and death, how it was, how the family and friends behaved, what are the real conventions governing a hopeless situation, and in what ways individuals interpret these conventions in their own style. . . .

I fear the world would say, He is cold, he is hardhearted. I particularly fear that mother would be pained because of some of the things I should have to say. But that particular fear may also be a disguise: I see, for example, that its benevolence conceals a certain grudge against my mother; it might be saying, very softly, If only she would die too. . . .

That is an embarrassing thing to have to say. It may even be the fear of having to say things of that sort which correctly identifies the fear which is my general subject: In some way, I want the world to think me a nice fellow, while I know I am not.

There is another form the fear takes, and this is or seems to be purely literary. At its loftiest, which it isn't very often, it refers to a hope to do nothing unworthy, nothing common or mean. For after all, one says, there are enough professional writers available to keep the world supplied with the standard product. There are many quite competent authors who, beginning with a touch of originality, have gone on to standardize (and maybe also refine) their kind of thing by doing more and more of the same. One is divided between the desire to keep on working, to *be* working, which is a condition usually of happiness and difficulty at once, and a desire to do only significant work, only work which is *necessary*. Hence this purely literary fear, which has also its many ridiculous, snobbish, and petty aspects. (One might write a funny novel about a novelist for whom no idea is good enough—a species of Henry James so much refined beyond the original one that he never wrote anything at all.)

One form of this resistance is the tedium belonging to the idea of 'the novel' itself; you say wearily, and with a superiority not entirely earned, To do all *that* again, describe the furniture, provide these people with different noses. . . .

And to a certain extent this attitude of boredom is essential if one is to be an artist at all: to have a keen nose for what has even barely begun to stink.

And in this attitude it is necesary to admit an objective factor not purely dependent upon the fear from within: There are so many novels! If Stendhal could shrink from the thought of autobiography because it would be obligatory to say *je* and *moi* such a number of times (he shrank; but he wrote the autobiography), consider how that kind of objection has grown in force in our day, when to write in the first person will give you the somewhat limited option of sounding like castoff Proust or Mike Hammer. There is, in fact, so much Literature that even the simplest and most natural expressions might have to be condemned because they have a faint flavor of Style: "I opened the door."

The fear of being ridiculous from want of knowledge. Being perfectly at home with the details of a herring fishery, a coat and suitery, a modern hospital, may be a very humble sort of art, but there it is; what do you do about it? Do you 're-search' it? The heart cools off at the word. Modern life has produced a vast number of specializations, and specialization perhaps has more essentially to do with the look and feel of life than it ever did before. The point perhaps is this: not that you must study up the professionalisms of your subject, but that the imagination must be afire, giving one a sufficient confidence to get along with the work. (It is my repeated experience that one knows many more relevant details than one is aware of before beginning; but how useless to begin without feeling even the possibility of being at home in the milieu.)

It begins now to appear, a little more bravely than at first, that I am listing my disqualifications for doing 'the ordinary novel,' the average novel that certain ball-point pens could write three of under water. But is there something else? Am I able to imagine something else? Apart from my laziness, which is not inconsiderable, I have a prior objection to doing something which will be put together out of technical tricks.

There comes a time in life—or there may come several such times—at which it appears necessary to ask yourself what you are doing. The question has to be put in a number of its aspects, for example, How did you get into this? What did it mean to you when you began? Does it still mean the same? Above all, perhaps, What is the secret meaning of 'writing'? For secret meaning it must have, to involve you during so many days, so many months, so many years, in this nearly exact balance of the wish by the fear, which makes you spend your time considering your inability to do just what you most wish to do.

At a certain age, anyhow, theory takes over. And this is nothing to be scared of, only you must go through it, not around it.

(Approaching this point, after having written these few pages foregoing, I experience a certain boredom and fatigue, which may be natural enough but may also be the first expression of resistance to what has to be said. O cursed spite. . . .)

When I began to be interested in literature (last year of high school), and when I began to wish to be a writer (first year in college), that area of human endeavor had the mantle of a grand glamor thrown about it. I remember that my friends and I regarded writing as essentially a religious mystery, and delighted ourselves with our presumption in believing the poet more blessed than the saint, as well as more powerful to bless.

In a glum and prosy, unglamorous manner, I continue to believe the same, remaining of the opinion that Mozart's life and work express a purer and more efficacious benevolence to humankind than the life and work of God.

But something has happened to this theme, whether in myself or in the world at large, or in both at the same time. Yeats speaks of coming into the desolation of reality, and this is for him a religious condition; it may be like what is intended by another splendid phrase of his, about withering into truth. But there is perhaps a prosier desolation of reality than that: In middle life, you perceive as though suddenly what was always there to be perceived, that all the stories are only stories. Beyond the stories, beneath them, outside the area taken account of by stories, there are the sickbed, the suffering, the hopeless struggle, the grave. It makes the stories look like hypocrisy, and the vision is so terrible that one becomes humbly grateful for the hypocrisy.

Now it is not impossible that this desolation of reality, which has always represented a crisis for the individual (see for example Tolstoy's marvelous and appalling *Confession*), has overtaken the world altogether, or so much of it as is available to my very limited view. Immense expansion of certain kinds of knowledge, certain kinds of power, has the effect of making the entire human past appear more than usually vain, limited, parochial, and trivial. Perhaps this can be expressed briefly by aphorism:

> It is according to the nature of life that Papageno should be helped on his way by a hideous old crone on condition that he will marry her. And it is according to the nature of love that when he agrees she will turn into a beautiful young girl. But it is according to the nature of art that both the hideous crone and the beautiful girl are played and sung by the same moderately pretty woman of a certain age, who has spent her youth learning music.

Or you might say: A life of universality and great generality is almost necessarily a skeptical life; belief is always necessarily parochial. Goethe added something sensible, to this effect, that the attitude of belief is fertile, while the attitude of skepticism is sterile—and that this remains true even if one is compelled to skepticism by the period in which one lives.

Just now, noticing in the last page a certain deplorable tendency to Style, to Eleganz, and all that Fancy Dan sort of thing, I think to put these reasonings by for a bit. But first these notes.

I was like Siddartha setting forth, who had never seen a poor man, a sick man, a dead man. But I was twice Siddartha's age.

If the choice were freely and simply given me, whether I would rather do one thing absolute, something on the order, say, of *Don Quixote*, or all the *Tom Swift* books, I perhaps would choose the latter, on the ground that it is best to live a busy life.

Reflexions—C

Obvious enough that generalities work to protect the mind from the great outdoors; is it possible that this was in fact their first purpose?

No matter how often and how far you digress, no matter how many clever improvisations you make to put off the exploration of your difficulty, or your impossibility; so long as you keep patiently bringing yourself back. Like that path through the Park, which rambled aimlessly but brought you out in front of the dentist's office anyhow.

Otherwise put: This process represents something also about the means of narration, which will not be linear and consecutive but will proceed by a series of fresh assaults on the center, each followed by its own drawing-back. These notes are notes about beginning, always beginning again. Plato said, The beginning is a god who while he lives among men redeems all.

Remember always that if you never wrote another line the world would not be poorer.

An essential element in the fear of writing is the fear of being thought unhappy, inadequate to the demands of being, what they call 'maladjusted.' Fear of being thought *weak*.

The emotion many of us believe proper to weakness—sickness, failure, *losing*—is shame, or embarrassment. A friend who had a heart attack wrote to me that what he chiefly felt was humiliation, as though he had let down some worthy cause. I used to observe about poker, for example, and have seen it in other games as well, that losing would helplessly be looked on by the loser as a defect of his character. Perhaps the same is true of 'being unable to write.' But you must continue an analysis of this sort dialectically: The shameful defect comes from some depth, it must be looked on as necessary, or desired; it punishes, but it punishes justly, or is felt by the sufferer to do so.

As well as having its religiously exalted mystique, writing was for me at the beginning sinful and a transgression. That is to say, the emphasis I place to this day on work, on being industrious for the sake of being industrious, contains a guilty acknowledgment that I became a writer very much against the will of my father, who wanted me to go into his business, or, as it used to be called, go to *work*. Of course, a large part of my effort must have gone into showing my father that I was nevertheless a man of good character, that art was just as much work as work was, &c. So by at one and the same time stressing the idea of work and being unable to work, it may be that I express my father's dominant will, and in a real sense am "going about my father's business." That is, the punishment of myself for separation; what he used so often to speak of, as of some strange medico-legal phenomenon he didn't quite understand, as "estrangement."

Even in writing to myself on this subject, I should acknowledge that these psychoanalytic pieties ought to be somewhat offset by remembering how much work I have got done in spite of my difficulties, or because of them. One doesn't know, it is true, how much work is par for the course (it is another of my weaknesses, that I keep nervously measuring my life against theoretical demands, continually make frightened comparisons, and generally regard the world far too exclusively as if it were a school). Consider the acknowledgment as made; yet the point here is not congratulation on the past any more than it is despair of the future; it is to seek a way through.

Thinking of my father in relation to my work reminds me of another factor which has some bearing on the true subject, fear. This is money, or the combination of money and worldly success, reputation, or even, if there is such a thing, true fame; what the Shakespeare children used to refer to rather smoothly as immortality.

For many years I made almost nothing by writing, and remember being ashamed of this when I had to provide information on this subject for my father's tax lawyers, who for reasons connected with his financial arrangements prepared my returns. Shame and the father again, I see without much surprise.

But then I began being able to sell poems for such sums as ten dollars (*The Nation*) or even a hundred (*The New Yorker*). This was fun, and I easily learned to regard sums of that kind as the sort of money Dr. Johnson said a man was seldom more harmlessly engaged than in making (I like that construction). And I would write reviews and essay-reviews for the quarterly magazines which from my college days I had identified, incorrectly, with literature in our time; for such things I might get as much as two hundred dollars. The general principle, which I formulated much later in conversation with my friend P, said that money is for cigarettes and whiskey, not for owning hotels and railroads.

Nor did my first two novels make any substantial change in my situation; I had an advance of a thousand dollars on each, and never made it up.

This reminds me, parenthetically, of all those brave spirits in college—myself I suppose included —who swore they would never *sell their souls* (expression of 1940) to Hollywood, &c., being at the time rather charmingly unaware how difficult a thing to sell was a soul; though some have at least succeeded in renting theirs out.

My third novel, though, while in its condition qua book it did not sell more than a mediocre run of copies, was translated and exalted from book to 'package,' and as a package it did, on Broadway and in Hollywood, modestly handsome. Not enough to qualify me as starting one of the great writing fortunes by any means, but enough to be quite beyond anything I had imagined. All one winter and spring my shoulder ached from carting those checks to the bank, and for six years thereafter there came every January some six to seven thousand dollars from the movie. Since I continued to earn my living otherwise than by writing, this success at once put me beyond the need of thinking about money. It is no contradiction, though, to add that I have thought much more about money since that time.

Now I do not abnormally dislike money, neither do I abnormally covet the stuff. Yet these rather large sums, even though they pleased me as putting on a more secure basis a life that had not essentially changed in style, even though they served me as evidence of success in the world my parents knew, may have caused me some uneasiness in respect of the relation among art, work, and reward. Perhaps I had remained all my life, though the child of rich people, naïvely persuaded that money was substantively a living wage more or less justly proportioned to effort and achievement, and not a speculative or magical triumph (any more than a disaster with the same adjectives). It would be absurd to ascribe my failure to write a novel since that time to this circumstance alone, or even, maybe, to this circumstance regarded as an important one. Yet I am sure it had its part to play along with many other considerations: While by far the largest part of my attitude to fortune was in favor of it as a grand convenience making for a certain independence of life, some small part stood stubbornly against it as an evidence, to say the least, of a frightening capriciousness in the relation between work and pay.

I think it is fair to say that I have worked for the work's sake, and not for the money. But I was able to see how easy it would be to become a writer who worked for the money, and it may be that I looked at my character as insufficiently strong or honest to stand closely beside that temptation for very long. That was not the only reason for my turning from that time more and more to poetry, but it was one of the reasons, or, rather, one of the causes, for I didn't reason all that out until much later.

A similar reaction was much more dramatically suffered by a friend, who, upon and as a response to the success of her most recent novel (best seller, sold to the movies), passed several months afraid to go out of the house, see people; she let the garbage accumulate on the porch, &c.

It is true, now I think of it, that this friend was to a certain extent acting out the subject of the novel itself, which had to do with a big house in a village, a family so hated by the folk that the girl feared to go shopping.

The analysis relating to money may be continued in application to other brands of success: reputation, fame, respect of one's peers first, and after that of the public.

I remember a poet's writing to me several years back, You are at present the most underrated poet in the country. But then, he added, that's better than being the most overrated poet in the country. I was and remain impressed by the short distance between the two extremes.

And I said once to F, Considering to what an extent we get into this business out of vanity and a hankering after fame, a wish to be loved by all the people, it is remarkable how very badly we respond to it when it begins to happen.

Maybe only four or five years ago, after seven books, I was absolutely neglected; then it began to happen, and now, after ten books, I am practically a pillar of the church, or ruined temple, of poetry. It is like being the respected proprietor of an industry making, to the highest standards of craftsmanship, a product which has just been superseded by something more modern. Some of the old folks will go on buying it out of piety; cranks who are also interested in cottage industry, colonial Williamsburg, and the preservation of monuments prefer it to the far more convenient and inexpensive replacement, and someday it will be much in demand as an antique, or classic of our literature; meanwhile, the entire industry, captains and crooks together, is failing.

The exact taste of this small fame in our time would not be easy to describe, since everyone experiences it according to his own temperament, and presents to its situation the mask he considers appropriate and within his dramatic means. I guess the main divisions are three, The High Priests, The Nice Guys, and the Sansculottes, or Beats, or Beards. (Though a Beard may easily be a High Priest, it depends on the trim and the combing.) I suppose I am the Nice Guy type, I grin at people, I tell them funny things, I am almost utterly non-controversial, even nonpolitical. If you behave in this manner publicly, I've found, it is possible to say the most shocking, and even subversive, things, equally certain that they will have no effect and that people won't challenge them, for they are stubbornly persuaded of one's harmlessness, as well as, maybe, of a certain innocuous unreality in the whole subject and situation. I suspect, too, that audiences feel hostility, and respond in kind, primarily as a matter of appearance and tone, rather than substance. (A Communist, not identified in advance as such, and one who really quite liked people, could probably convert a good many, in a half-assed way, if he didn't mention the bad word itself.)

As has many times been said, you cannot make much money writing poetry, but you can make quite a fair lot of money talking to people about writing poetry. You sometimes get paid at movie star prices, though infrequently and for short periods; by assiduous application to the task, you could make your income rival that of a successful psychoanalyst, at least for a couple of years; my take for last year, from all sources, was just exactly what the Giants paid the best relief pitcher in the league. All this happens at some distance from La Bohème.

It is often contended, mostly by those who do it, that this sort of thing—lecturing, giving 'readings' (like a gypsy with tea leaves?), and teaching—is very harmful to the artist. I don't experience it in that way, for several reasons: It came to me late, when I was already very set in the forms of my devotion; I am of a somewhat cynical temper; I like to meet people, for short times, and rather enjoy getting out of the house, though I also enjoy getting back; I like teaching; I like being made much of, though not for very long, and commanding those ridiculously large sums of money is a sort of gaming pleasure. Most of all, that business has nothing to do with art, which takes place elsewhere and has quite other problems (analysis, communion, not imitating oneself, for instance).

But all these reasons are irrelevant, if you consider only the work to count. I am persuaded I could not work otherwise than as I do if I lived in a cave, and as for the quality of the work, that is not for me to judge.

And that may raise a point worth bothering with relative to the general theme of 'being unable to write.' I suspect what I have said applies, for me, chiefly or even exclusively to poetry, which is a solitary and introspective art for most of its practitioners. The novel might indeed demand a more explicit attention to the details of this world, especially the details of its people.

Also, if I take a certain pleasure in the being able to confront people, talk to them, and talk with them, that too has something to do with the parents: In early life I was most frequently criticized by my mother for being shy, sullen, uncommunicative.

Of course, all this lecturing is said by the pious to waste time as well as talent. True enough, one might spend that time at the desk—where I spent what look in retrospect to be uninterrupted years. But if one of my problems has been not writing enough, the other that matches it exactly is writing too much. The peculiar vexation I am trying to fix in these pages is not simply being unable to write, it is being unable for the past few years to write fiction. The subject divides itself into opposed halves: why should I want to do this? Why should it be so difficult, or impossible? (I *am* changing the subject; probably we are not through dealing with money and success. But just now I am bored with that, and I summon myself back to the beginning once again.)

I've spent most of the time on the second part of the question; now a little on the first. Why should I, after turning purposely to poetry alone some five years ago, and producing a large quantity of works in that area, feel so strong and helpless an impulse, almost compulsion, to write fiction, especially to write a novel?

I see one reason right off. It has to do with the upbringing once again. For a Jewish Puritan of the middle class, the novel is serious, the novel is work, the novel is conscientious application—why, the novel is practically the retail business all over again. But poetry is exalted pleasure, and in the world of my childhood and adolescence, pleasure is primarily known as something that has to be paid for.

A characteristic metaphor for this division has occurred to me many times: The novel is marriage. Poetry is infidelity. I thought of this first with respect to the steady, long-term involvement with the one as against the violent suddenness and intermittence of the other; but it may apply in other ways as well.

A second reason. One must, as a duty, take time off from poetry. It may be true that a style is made by sedentary toil, and by the imitation of great masters, but that is a long time ago, for me, and besides, I too seek an image, not a book. This past year I have sought the needed relief in essays speculating on the meaning of poetic art.

Those speculations seem to me a necessity if one is to continue developing in one's work; and there is a fascinating theme here, to which I shall return later on, debating the extent to which speculation has in the past couple of decades visibly begun to replace art; how much the making challenges artistic interest more than what is made; how art as adventure seems for the present almost to have overthrown the work of art. Later on.

One takes time off from poetry, not, I hope, to do fiction slightly or slightingly, though there remains the idea that the crises of development in poetry happen in the silence, and when one attends for a long time to something else. But there is also this to be said: Lyric poetry, just because of its great refinement, its subtlety, its power of immense implication in a confined space—a great reckoning in a little room—is perpetually in danger of preferring gesture to substance. It thins out, it goes through the motions, it shows no responsibility. I conceive this responsibility of poetry to be to great primary human drama, which poets tend to lose sight of because of their privilege of taking close-ups of single moments on the rim of the wheel of the human story. The poet will improve his art who acknowledges the necessity of always returning to that source; he will fail who always writes another poem instead. Hence it has seemed to me that I must attempt to bring together the opposed elements of my character represented by poetry and fiction. The novel is of course not the only means of doing this, for there exist these alternatives: poetic drama, drama in prose, narrative, epic, and philosophic poetry. All have to do with expanding the framework and the ambit of feeling. All, except the second, have in modern times a great air of absurdity, too, and unreality; you would need a stocking cap, maybe a wig, a quill pen. . . . *The Testament of Beauty* is a noble attempt, and there is some true eloquence in it, but Bridges comes nowhere near encompassing the delineation of modern thought, perhaps an impossible object to begin with. *The Dynasts* is a monstrous attempt to meet a monstrous situation: history. The *Cantos* is a mess. True, and tempting, that Valéry himself proposed *The Intellectual Comedy* as a greater work than either the *Divine* or the *Human* . . . and Coleridge said to himself that he would expect to read for ten years and compose for five! Very likely it is true, as it is often said, that nowadays prose says it better over the long distance; Tolstoy manages with a certain appearance of ease the confrontation with great events that Hardy doesn't, quite.

And yet poetry acknowledges noble and even impossible ambitions, though perhaps at the end there emerges from the mountain only a transcendently powerful mouse: you might have to write A *Vision* in order to write A *Needle's Eye*, *Jerusalem* in order to say "Truly, my Satan, thou art but a dunce."

But, alas—and this alas is thematic—what do great works signify? What is the human story? and has it the former interest, the former passion? The great powers of the day are powers of patient, minute analysis; in the realm of the highest eros man shows mostly impotence.

There is a sickness of literature, too, a surfeit and a sickness. To believe in the human story, to love the human story—how unsophisticated, parochial, maybe even sinful. Better to behave like an ant, that is, a patient specialist responsible for statements of great precision in precisely limited situations, never for the whole, or the wholeness of things.

But all this is getting very fancy and far away.

REFLEXIONS—D

Suppose a man inhabited by ghosts. What are these ghosts? Pathetic incompetents, for the most part, revenants who don't know the way back; a good phrase for them would be what M applied to certain artists: would-be has-beens. They manifest themselves as fractions of people—a name, the gesture of a hand, a certain set of the mind, some half-remembered bending of the neck in lamplight indicating consent. They appeal, at their poor best of ability, to the man to bring them back. But there are two major obstacles in the way. First, that any one of them can be brought back only at the expense of many others, whose fragments must be taken from them and given to the chosen one, to complete him sufficiently to be visible. Second, the man fears these pleaders; that they can live only at each other's expense is to him a sign that given the power they will live at his expense, and overwhelm him. But at the same time the man constantly says that their existence alone can complete and confirm his own existence; it is by their being that he is.

For many years he temporizes with the poor ghosts, pretending to debate which of them shall live again and which must be sacrificed to that end. But this is only pretense, even though the man often succeeds in fooling himself as well as the ghosts; his real purpose is to keep them in their subordinate, incomplete, and powerless state of neither being nor not being: *divide et impera*. This solution at least assures his superiority, but over what?

One Latin tag deserves another, so it may be said that this man is like a Holy Roman Emperor placed in authority over squabbling realms: *et Caesar et nihil*.

What this man is running is certainly a fraud. But he is its victim as well as its manipulator, for these ghosts are pieces of his past inward to him, striving and crying to issue into the world again; weak masters though they are, they will hurt him if they can't do this.

The haunted man observes concerning the last few phrases that they contain in a triple figure the three meanings of birth, excrement, and pustulant infection; the ghosts are his children, shit, the matter of his sickness. Also, that his high regard for the greatest possible possibility, or potential, as somehow preferable to most or all realizations —you can have more ghosts if you allow none of them fully to return—betrays a radical conservatism (or constipation?) in his nature; you might call it a youthful virtue now turning into a middle-aged vice. He wants to keep his world, and fears to give it away; consequently it has begun to fester inside him.

The final turn to the above brilliant analysis is that the man hasn't the least idea whether any of it is true.

There is, too, a fourth meaning added to the other three: death. The man fears to liberate or objectify his own spirit, seeing this 'giving away' as contradictory to his selfishness, that is, his desire to keep on being himself. So the improvisation of the past few minutes brings him round to a paradox which is also a platitude: Trying to save his soul, he loses it.

Also: The

parable of the incapable novelist persistently attempts to be about God's imperfect creation of Man.

There is something poetically, artistically, traditionally, satisfying to such writings as the above. That's the way it used to be done, isn't it? The tale, the anecdote, the situation, progressively yielding its treasures of perhaps false information, its harmonic relations among several different levels—the power is not in any particular depth to the thoughts, for the deepest human thought is not much removed from the shallowest, but in the steepness of the gradient from one thought to another—proceeding through irony to paradox, emerging in the brilliant combination of tragic impossibility with conventional piety, the identity of moral, trope, and anagoge. . . . A very pretty bit of work. One suspects it is done almost entirely by language, without the intervention of a living human intelligence at all.

The Novelists. A small group of people, each of whom is writing his or her first novel. They all know that they are writing about one another, under different names, in different situations—which may well be, however, slight variations of the literal and physical situation known by all to exist among them—and they are all jealous of their secrets, the secrets of style and information (gossip). A professional novelist lives nearby, and because they are snobs each of them applies to this man (woman?) for criticism, advice, and, above all, praise. The professional novelist, who has been searching for a possible novel to write, writes their novels as one novel. But this one novel is esesntially an account of the process just set forth in this paragraph, the coming to know. The novelists gradually become aware of what is happening to them, that they are becoming people in a novel. Their behavior changes radically because it is now conditioned by the presence of their novelist ("Have you met our novelist?" asked Frances), who in his turn is affected by the change so that the novel becomes impossible to fix on paper; perhaps at last he suffers a breakdown and has to be taken away, leaving the others feeling a trifle lost. For as Ortega said, Man is the novelist of himself.

There was a rather cruel game they used to play, or not only a game but an initiation rite, since it required the presence of one person unacquainted with its secret. The exoteric rite, told to the newcomer, gave the rules of the game thus: You go out of the room while we make up a story. Returning, you are required to get the story out of us by asking questions which may be answered only by Yes or No. But in the esoteric version known to all the old hands, no story was made up. If the key word in the question began with a letter A-M, the answer would be yes. If it began with N-Z, the answer would be no. So the poor player, on returning to the circle of friends, would with less and less tentativeness (as well as with increasing pride in his investigative skill) expose by means of these arbitrary replies some things about his own being which he might have preferred to keep hidden.

And here is a characteristic first reaction, after ten minutes, to possibility: Is it possible? Where is the energy coming from to keep this mess stirred up? Isn't it far too complex? Finally —at the best, everyone will say it is a tour de force; brilliant but not serious. What they will say at the worst I hesitate to consider.

They tried this game on Felix when he first came among them. But although he didn't know the trick he suspected there was one, and he was protected by his professional vanity as well. On going out of the room he said to himself that of course they were going to 'make up' one of his novels, and the joke would be that he couldn't find it out by asking questions. So on returning he decided to make them tell the latest one if he could, and if he couldn't, their replies would indicate which of the earlier ones they meant. So he began with the plot of *The Crooked Eclipses,* and got through it fairly well on the ground that when an answer didn't quite meet his expectation that meant only that the person answering hadn't read the book, or hadn't read it with sufficient attention, or had forgotten it.

But they tried it later on, on a young man who was going to marry one of the daughters, and it broke up the marriage. At the very least.

Reflexions—E

Hypothesis. The novel is about disclosure of secrets. The best secrets combine two secret realms: sex (generation) and money. Maybe the ideal is attained in a novel by Ivy Compton Burnet, where the ward sleeps with his guardian's new young wife and begets upon her the male child who will replace him as the heir.

Maybe there are no secrets. The novelist is in the position of the professional blackmailer whose prospective victims simply won't care: Look at the Kinsey report, they tell him, What's there that everyone doesn't know?

But it is nonsense to say that there are no more secrets. The supposed candor of modern talk about sex may well be the handsomest disguise in the world for bravely avoiding the painful realities of this theme. And there is a great deal of financial prudishness, too. Power increasingly has its secrets; what novelist has tackled the imaginative problem of how decisions really get made? C. P. Snow? Well.

It might even get to the sticky point of assassination, just to save the company embarrassment. The funniest thing would be the scene showing everyone's extreme aversion from talking about that; finally they would have to invent a whole language for the purpose, a language of graceful abstractions such as "interdict" and "rearrange."

A family firm engaged in making certain large machines for the government. A liberal son and daughter. The machines turned out to be gas chambers.

Anecdote heard last night: A young scion of the radical Right falls in love with a Negro girl. Perhaps the real story here would be about his father. "Creeping sentimentality."

Reflexions—F

Looking over for the first time in sequence what I have written of this supposed self-examination, some critical thoughts come to me; many of them might begin, Listen, you little son of a bitch. . . .

Characteristically, a strong and single impulse breaks up into a dozen 'ideas,' none of which can be selected in preference to another.

Toward the beginning, I recognized my evasions and brought myself back; but further on, evasion became the order of the day. I allowed, that is to say, my resistances to express themselves in the guise of 'Ideas.'

There is an extraordinary amount of self-justification going on in the pages relating to money, presenting the amusing spectacle of a man ready to admit to cowardice, extreme self-ishness, and artistic impotence, but at the same time unable to forgive himself for a comfortable income.

Writing fiction is much simpler than I make out. One maxim I recall to have accompanied those attempts which succeeded at least in the degree that I finished them, was this: You are not asking the reader to like it, you are ramming it down his throat.

And perhaps even self-examination, analysis, all production of general ideas, thought itself, are in the end evasions of a story.

Stories that attract me quite regularly have to do with fraud. Debasement and counterfeit especially of the intellectual and artistic currency a subject of great charm. Hence a novel about a forged painting, another about a cartel of ghost writers who provide an immense part of all the poetry and fiction done in the country.

      The novel about the forged painting, "The Kiss of Judas" by someone very like La Tour, was to express also a certain possible fraudulence to history itself, to the idea of the past by which we believe we live. Probable that notions of this kind mean to express in secrecy my belief that I too am a fraud. So in one of my books a man wrote himself anonymous letters in order to get 'reality' to make the next move.

Bill Troy once wrote of Balzac that the novelist and the criminal are both interested in conspiracies, that is, in plots. So that when Balzac wrote of Vautrin there was a fruitful symbiosis between subject and method.

The heroes I think of are far from heroic; typically, they are diffident, ironic, or timorous of the world, and have only so much energy as will enable them to make one tentative move and then wait for the world to say what it thinks of that. It may be now that I should deliberately affront and shock myself by dreaming a monster of energy and vile ambition, someone who invents his plot as he goes along simply by upsetting everything, by bustling. Someone who makes others suffer as an affirmation of his own life. For what one imagines as in every way the opposite of oneself will shrewdly turn out also to be oneself.

For it is the possibility of operation of fiction that the phantastic idea of 'character' enables us to believe in our own being by radical simplifications; perplexed because we know ourselves confusedly to be Everyman, we are temporarily pleased to view ourselves as Someman, even accepting his villainy or foolishness if necessary in order to gain at the same time this soothing sense of identity, of living within limits where all is known.

Away, then, with this collection of schlemihls who have preempted my dreams for so many years! I see instead cold and somber men, implacably embittered by life, cruel of will and subtle of mind. They are selfish, energetic, and utterly lost, and they run the world. And as soon as I say this I see that I too am that.

Reflexions—G

There are powers of superior force and powers of superior guile. Apart from these, there is the power of love, which works without making a move. There is a sort of judo of the will. Applied guilt is a great lever.

A young girl is saved from drowning by a stranger. Later, he tries to make love to her, and she manages to put him off by a lie: She says that she had been trying to drown herself. This lie has two effects: It binds her in thought to him, as someone the lie has obligated her to make up to, and it fixes his passion for her, making it exclusive, love supervening on lust. Over the protests of her parents, he marries her, they go away to live in a far country, in a castle by the sea, and there he makes her so unhappy that she drowns herself. He is, by the way, a skin diver. His name is Andrea. A girl something like J, who writes of an older man, "he is just sadistic and arrogant enough to satisfy all sorts of crazy things inside me for a few weeks." Less intelligent than J would still be intelligent enough.

REFLEXIONS—H

Now there, with the emergence of a workable-looking story, appears the chance of analysis I began this for. Never mind that the analysis itself is a way of avoiding the story; I admit that. But I have the feeling that something has to be faced before I can go on.

The first part of this story came to me several years ago, and without much thought I did the beginning of the first scene as a comedy; the boy was a plebeian, and 'utterly unsuitable.' So perhaps it's as well that those pages, and the notes I did after them, are not around (probably burned). But to have failed once at the idea is an obstacle. I think I have only once completed a prose fiction many times attempted, and that was a fable.

A contradiction: This story remained pleasurably lively in the mind since yesterday morning, and was still there this morning. At the same time, I feel the usual terror of beginning it.

Reasons for this terror? Laziness is surely one. What a great weight one adds to the heart by simply saying, "It was a fine morning in summer." Lack of knowledge is another. There is so much I don't know that I would have to pretend to know at the start, and hope to make up later. Perhaps the solution to this difficulty is to continue for a while toying with the phantasies which have come into my head in such numbers since I first put down the subject.

Related difficulty: how to keep this story from involving itself with so many other stories; scrupulous avoidance of opportunities for 'getting in' this that and the other. Similarly, the character of the girl has got to be kept clear, and not mixed with the characters of other girls thought of as in other situations.

The big reason, which presents itself as nontechnical (hence more terrifying) is that I am afraid to write about love, and afraid to write about sex. Why? Afraid of showing my ignorance, not of what people do, but the tone of what they do; afraid to be stilted, priggish, inept, afraid on the other hand of wallowing.

But you can convert this into a technical difficulty by the consideration that this ignorance you impute to yourself is world-wide. The first axiom of the novelist is: Nobody in the world knows how the world is. It follows that one guess is as good as another. You don't ask the reader's consent, you impose upon him with your phantasy. Perhaps it would relieve you to begin with the premise that the world of your fiction is a nonrepresentational world, or at any rate an abstract one in which specific distortions in the interest of vision are not merely permissible but a requirement. If you believe—and I have heard you say you do—that most novels do not seem to you to represent the soul with any great degree of fidelity to its truth, surely it is open to you to attempt some slightly different way of revealing the beast. Perhaps your novel, the one for which you have, as you say, *an idea*, would be mostly analytic, as these pages are, the not necessarily temporal exploration of the motives of the heart. You might begin as one would a sermon or a fugue, with the abstract statement of the subject, the text, the 'what happened' which is of interest only as it reflects the why and how of happening.

It is to be expected that my characters, coming from the head of a monster—but a monster extremely introspective and able to penetrate human disguises by sympathy—would be criticized as being monstrous, as being not 'real human beings.' I expect many of us, but book reviewers first, would run screaming from the sight of a real human being.

Book reviewers have got from much reading a clear impression of what life is like; this clear impression they professionally apply to showing that the books they read are not lifelike.
That
could be a good deal better phrased. But so.

My novel would take up, something most novels avoid by definition, the problem of memory. The novelistic convention says that memory is not a problem for the character, not a problem for the writer, not a problem for the reader. With practically no exceptions, what is put down on the paper is by convention the duplication of what happened.
But I would
make this precisely the question, and precisely my novel. My book consists of the vision and analysis of moments: the moment at which the girl is saved from drowning (not described at the time, but by her unsatisfactory memory of it: a green, cold confusion, a being ignominiously lifted up and turned over as for a spanking, a sense of sick lassitude and muscular weakness supervening even upon wild fear), the moment later that night in which she lies about the first moment; the moment a year or more later when she goes to destroy herself.

It might be of the nature of this narration that it had only the briefest scenes. It occurs exclusively in someone's mind, hers, his; and since the story is being told in part by her mind, it is possible that the drowning at the end never happened at all, but is a fable she has made up to express something about her life.

The briefest scenes; like epigrams in their character.

Since your problem is a universal problem, you could also give it a technical nature, and so go far toward solving it, by making it the girl's problem too. She knows, if that is possible, less about the world than you do.

Best of all, it is a story with no apparent symbolic meaning. It's just plain something that happened, interesting to tell for the reason that its beginning and end look to be related; is this relation fortuitous, or what? Is there such a thing as pure accident, or does what seems accidental express will, human or other, or fate, or design, or art?

The crucial thing, literally, is that he destroys her faith. She was brought up in the Episcopal Church, and has never much questioned the matter. More positively than that, she believes in God, something not easy to represent. As for him, he is a renegade Catholic, who keeps his defection private for family reasons (his inheritance) until he has this girl and the bit of money she brings him.
                    Now here is the opportunity of a double attack. He destroys her faith, but in doing so cannot avoid revealing his own atheism, and he is disinherited. After this, he turns to smuggling, under the appearance of an expedition diving for sunken treasure. Something like this makes the middle action, which I was in doubts about.

It is a funny, engaging, and pathetic trait of the mind that this story may look impossible tomorrow, dull, stupid, not worth telling. But today it seems to concentrate mysterious riches, and the probable reason for this is what I said a moment ago: no apparent symbolic meaning; which means that I do not know the symbolics of it; which is a good position to be in at the start of any adventure.

Here is a beginning.

When Betty Lord was saved from drowning, one fine July afternoon, her parents responded by having a few people over for drinks at five, and invited the young man, the foreign young man, who had done the saving.

I see a third figure, have seen him for some hours now, an American boy who had been 'in love with' Betty. He will appear again at the three-quarter mark for an interlude that provokes the crisis.

It was not so much riches, Betty thought, as the cleanliness of riches, the white, sweet New England houses where the grounds were so beautifully kept one never had to think of them as being made of dirt. Riches and filth together, well, it was not an idea she had ever had to consider.

First resistances begin to appear: a certain weariness, feeling the story is both thin and obvious, also that half of it has to be set in Europe or the Caribbean, about either of which I know nothing. I remind myself that local color is not the object, the object is to tell the story. But I can see that much in me is against the telling of this or any other story, and probably this much can't always be fought but has to be sometimes also cajoled, amused, hypnotized . . . or else a place must be found in the story itself for whatever it is in me that doesn't want the story told.

One way to do this: During the story there is an interlude, in which Betty meets and talks with a tourist, who happens also to be a novelist; her novelist, though this is never mentioned.

All this never happened, but it is essential to be accurate about how.

REFLEXIONS—I

Who are you? Well, I was born in 19— in —— City. I attended —— School and —— College, receiving my degree in 19—. During the War I served in the —— Army. I married and had — children. Have worked for the following firms ——, ——, ——. Yes, but who are you? ——?

Aristotle said that character is revealed only in action. He is perfectly correct, I guess, if by character we stress the moral nature, which perhaps only Christianity pretends to judge in independence of actions. But the novelist as a rule deals with more quotidian people than Aristotle's dramatists did, and it is the definition of character for such people that they do not enact 1 per cent of what is in them; if they enacted, say, 2 per cent, they would be bankrupt, in jail, or dead. Therefore the novelist must to some extent deal with dreams, but to what extent does he deal with dreams as though they were realities? as though people did act them out?

                  This has become a most interesting theme very recently, mostly I think because of the very large and unsophisticated audience it is possible for the novelist to have; people whose notion of 'realism,' derived from the movies, includes a large symphony orchestra playing the dramatis personae about their business.

            In these circumstances, it is easily possible for the

phantasies of adolescents during masturbation to become the reality of a decade later.

An anecdote I read as one term of an analogy the other day: In Victorian times, in England, white slavery flourished precisely because it was forbidden to be talked about; the innocence of the young ladies made them an easy prey, &c. The author went on to say that we should not similarly create a false innocence by refusing to contemplate nuclear warfare. Morally, I quite approve all this clear-sighted facing up to disagreeable realities. But I also incline to wonder whether any practical result, other than the pleasure of being clear-sighted, is envisioned. For probably Victorian society was ridden by homosexuality, too, and some would say for the same reason, that it could not be talked about except as a dramatic scandal such as the Wilde affair; that is, as the exception it wasn't. But has the freedom (first of novelists, later of most everyone) to discuss the existence of homosexuality made for less of it, or more? More important, has it made the homosexual's life better, easier, less haunted? Has this freedom essentially domesticated or civilized this form of life? Or does it remain, for its practitioners and for the others, an assertion of criminal intent with respect to society? the expression of a will, compelled or freely chosen, to the subversive and deviant?

The realism of a phantasied life—that is, its attention to detail chosen from everyday things given a sinister and archaic turn —may be less presently diagnostic than prophetic of the future. Perhaps no one could mistake Golding's fable of children for anything but parable. Kafka's *Trial*, on the other hand, presents its agon right in among the trivial furniture of town life, and its form of arrest, for example, if not a reality at the time of composition, became one shortly thereafter.

A good example of the process whereby art works on life, what might be jargoned up into 'the social realization of individual phantasy' is Ayn Rand's *Atlas Shrugged*. I spent a week last summer reading it, a week of coldly bored fascination, and do not plan on reading it again. But I would not be so professionally horrified by it as liberal reviewers generally were; I would rather distinguish this from that about it as follows.

The vision of the corruption and eventual paralysis of a civilization is an epic subject, and she does it, so far as concerns the picturesque, very handsomely. It is also in some way a natural, for we are all subversive enough to be taken with an image of The End, the mighty wheels grinding to a halt, and so on. And she sees convincingly the dependence of part on part, of some hugely unreckonable whole upon these many and intricate dependencies; she dramatizes the process with considerable descriptive force.

But then you come to her diagnosis of this phenomenon, and the accompanying claim, made right in the novel, that the America to which these things are happening is the real America you can see right out the window, and the whole dream reveals its absurdity. That the prosperity of so huge an enterprise should depend solely on the efforts of the half dozen richest people in the world who are at the same time its inventors, managers, and even composers, is plain silly,*

* plain silly, &c., above. Yes, but it has to be allowed that this silliness about life has its dramatic and compositional justifications. Even a novel about great wealth is permitted to be austerely economical in its means, and what Miss Rand does, from the point of view purely of making fictions, is nothing more than what is traditionally done in poetry and drama with royal and eponymous heroes who sum society in their persons, or for that matter what is done in the writing of history, where Napoleon 'did' this and Hitler 'did' that; or, for the matter of that, what is done in the making of history,

though perhaps less so than the symbolic peripety which makes the redemption of the world conditional upon the heroine's getting laid by the worker-king between the tracks beneath Grand Central.

Now this book is intended no less practically than Dante intended the *Comedy,* to get those souls out of the muck and into glory. And from it have been derived both a 'philosophy' and a 'school,' with a disciple to expound, with the authority of some questionably interpreted Aristotle, with the manners of Stalinists or the dedicated members of a Gestapo novitiate.

To be scrupulous, one should add that Dante's machinery doesn't look any less silly than Miss Rand's. And people spent a vast deal of time believing in Dante's machinery, or something very like it. And the world went on its way from one disaster to the next, as usual.

All this tends to assert that if you tried to say why the *Divine Comedy* is a great work and *Atlas Shrugged* a poor work you would find yourself in difficulties, which you might probably attempt to get out of either by appeal to formalism (Dante is so skillful at riming) or by appeal to truth (Dante shows what human beings are really like. But does he? Or, rather, how do you happen to know? from reading Dante?).

It is a related problem that the novel seems increasingly unable to avoid referring to the particular-historical. I do not mean only what Toynbee remarks, that 'fiction' is characteristically played out in a space which is nine-tenths non-fictional; which is scarce more than to say that Claudius' fic-

where a huge Pharaoh slaughters hordes of tiny Hittites, or where the head of a great state is credited with the formulation of its biological theory, art criticism, and so on.

tional bottom is applied to the seat of a perfectly real throne. No, I mean the tendency I have seen for novels to have their stories conditioned directly by historical event. *The Fox in the Attic, A Favorite of the Gods,* Anthony Powell's series.

Whenever I try to make a distinction it is sure to collapse. Does history enter into the books just named otherwise than it does when Napoleon enters into *War and Peace* or the Dreyfus Case into *À la recherche?* I just don't have any idea.

You can see how human beings get into trouble when they try to think; the requirements of a complex head and a simple heart possibly exclude each other. Or as a Jesuit said it: "A finite being with an intellect is always too smart for himself." (Walter Ong.)

Perhaps the above analyses mean to demonstrate only the futility of analysis, that is the application of intelligence to questions of human import which are passive and nontemporal, hence subject only to choice, not to solution; which would bring us round in a circle again to action.

Any novelistic assertion I make that thus and such happened, or that the furniture in the room was disposed in a certain manner, contains the implicit preface: I assert that . . . meaning, either I choose to assert, or I am compelled to assert. The compulsion may come about initially from my own nature (fascination with drowning compels me to assert that Betty drowned, and that this was connected with her having nearly drowned at an earlier date), or, later on, from the consequences of what was asserted earlier.

The novelist imputes motives for happenings. He delineates characters, or appearances, such that these motives shall seem more or less plausible, but more than less inevitable.

When Betty Lord was saved from drowning, one brilliant afternoon in July, her mother and father met the situation by inviting a few friends over for drinks and to thank the young man, the handsome young foreigner, who had done the saving. I mention the matter chiefly because Betty later married this fellow, who took her away to his castle by the sea in a foreign land (it was his father's estate, in fact, on an island in the Caribbean Sea), and there made her so unhappy, the story goes, that she drowned herself.

But I have another reason for bringing it up. I was one of the few friends invited, and I am by trade a novelist and teller of stories—whether they be histories or lies. It meant something uncertain to me, to be present at the beginning of a series of events which led to an end so artistically like the beginning.

Apart from that—I was not in love with Betty, I scarcely knew Betty. I regret what happened to her, but this regret is composed somewhat impersonally of convention and the sorrows of poetry for quick bright things come to confusion.

I regret much, but my passion is to know. And since I cannot know I must imagine. I must imagine deeply, first into the life of a girl I scarcely knew, into the mind of a young man I somewhat admired but did not much like, into scenes and circumstances remote from my own . . . all of which, however, will at last return me to the imagining of my own imagination, which attempts to see these things.

REFLEXIONS—J

Situation for satiric farce. An extremely provincial business-
man who has long held views similar to those of the John
Birch Society but has been sensibly afraid to make much
public display of these; the changing temper of the country
gives him the illusion that these views of his make utter
sense, and responds to his illusion by actually giving him a
certain small, rising fame, the beginning of a party, or a
branch of the Republican party, a platform, especially money
and influence.

After the rise of our man and his organization
to some curious eminence, he discovers to his consternation
that a large part of his support comes from a few people who
really *are* Communists—paid by Moscow gold, &c. Well, he
knows he ought to go straight to the FBI and confess, so
as to be no more than a fool and not a real criminal, or
traitor. But he can't—because, evidently, dignity is the key
to these people, vainglory, pompousness, and a certain com-
placency beneath their cries of disaster. (Also, he is person-
ally sort of a nice guy, and he is in this with others.)

So that
is the first revelation. But behind it is a second revelation:
the Communist party these days is very largely run and sup-
ported by the FBI; four out of five members are estimated to
be informers. The realization that this is so might nearly
drive our boy insane with its mixture of peril and security

(you can't throw the FBI's people out of your organization just because they are pretending to be Communists pretending to infiltrate your right-wing group).

Still further back is the point of the joke, that the FBI members pretending to be Communists pretending to be American Vigilantes . . . are in there in all earnest, they really want to be American Vigilantes because that is their vision too of what life is like.

In the end it will be our boy's moderation and residual decency, his helpless belief in the civility of life, that bring him down off the high places. Or this is the way I tend to see him now; much would depend on how much of a son of a bitch he turned out to be as he (as I) went along.

You would see him starting out with 'a philosophy,' which amounted to a simple practical program; gradually being forced to improvise at an ever-increasing pace; his implicit view at the beginning, of civilization as a melodrama and spy story, would turn into a reality on him.

One notices that, unlike the last notion, of which it probably is an evasion, this one appears to contain *rien de personnel.* Its problems are for cold brilliance to solve, they require outrageousness. It would be a study in the extent to which an imagined world works on and replaces a real one. In the reality-conferring power of publicity. In the power of false art.

The big problem would be, as usual with satire, treating this with a straight face (for there is a satire behind the apparent one, of a novelist treating this theme and as a result joining the John Birch Society with full conviction); it can't be done as a private joke to be shared by intellectuals, you have to take your cranks and villains with utter seriousness. Ideally, a good many reviewers would read it as the straight goods, and if our Hero lost they would draw profound moral lessons from this about the decay of ancient virtues.

It's said that satire is no longer possible, the reality having outrun it, but I wonder if that need be so. It takes a good deal of energy, of course (one of my typical excuses, meaning, most likely, that it takes a single-mindedness and capacity to endure boredom which I simply do not have).

A new form of the idea. The novelist is in on the end as well as the beginning. The story is his, and his the expression of motive. The girl had said she was in love with *him,* and then came along the stranger who saved her from drowning.

Let it be that the stranger Andrea was introduced to this outfit by the novelist Felix; let it be that the stranger was a sort of rich-boy beginning novelist; let it be that Felix tells the story himself—as an idea for a novel he would like to write; let it be also that Betty's death is reported at first ambiguously and in connexion with deep-sea diving, so that it might have been an accident, and therefore let it be called in a deliberately melodramatic way *Rapture of the Depths.*

The novelist, with his power of giving life and taking it way.

This makes for a book intermediate between the first and the third, called *Speculations,* where in view of the end and the beginning Felix Ledger considers what most probably may have happened in the time intervening. Which saves this poor slave a good bit of faked-up Caribbean nonsense, with coral reefs and tropical fish.

There comes a time in a man's life at which the daughters of his friends appear to him the appropriate and impossible objects of his thought.

A man who can lie so convincingly about his own life should have no trouble telling the truth about the lives of others who do not exist.

But this story is a long way still from being ready to be written. You remark, of course, how the two utterly separate stories, this one and the one about The Novelists, show signs of wanting to come into phase. You warned yourself against that earlier on, yet it seems intrinsic to the idea of composition that they should—and that even the political satire thought of yesterday should strike a glancing light against the sides of the main object.

That may be a reason, too, for its taking me so long between one fiction and the next; not 'having an idea,' but having ten or twenty ideas, and having to wait as patiently as possible for the relations among them to reveal themselves.

Which puts me in mind of something I copied out of Freud seven years ago (the year in which I last wrote a novel): "the dreamer's associations begin by *diverging* widely from the manifest elements, so that a great number of subjects and ranges of ideas are touched upon, after which, a second series of associations suddenly *converge* from these on to the dream-thoughts that are being looked for."

It is that moment of convergence one has to wait for.

A moment earlier in the same essay, he says: "When the pressure of resistance is quite extremely high, one meets with the phenomenon of the dreamer's associations broadening instead of deepening. In place of the desired associations to the dream that has already been narrated, there appear a constant succession of new fragments of dream, which in their turn remain without associations."

I had remarked that this frequently happened in my experience of dreams. Each dream in itself would remain quite impenetrable to my probing for its sense, but instead of revealing its truth it would set off the memory of another dream, or a further fragment of the same one. As though the unconscious employed flattery to prevent me from understanding: Look how imaginative you are, how many dreams, how many images, all in one night!

Much the same thing appears to happen in the course of these notes, when the mind, unable to bear the richness of consequence entailed upon one idea, forthwith produces another instead.

BOOK TWO

I dreamed I had an extra ticket for *Don Giovanni*. There were three ways to walk to the opera house, and I congratulated myself on having used two of these ways on two previous visits, so that I still had a new way to take this time. When I got there the phone booth was occupied by a tall bald man. This annoyed me, because I wanted to phone ——— (in my class at high school) to offer her the extra ticket. When the bald man came out of the booth I went to phone, but suddenly awakened on the reflexion that after all ———, like myself, was well over forty years old by now, so what the hell.

I awakened in a condition of considerable sexual excitement (——— might take that as a pretty compliment these days, though she never did in high school), but also very scared. Something I remembered hours later. The extra ticket was one of three, not two. Something else: I kept remembering the opera first as *Tristan*, then realizing it was *Don Giovanni*.

Some of the structure of the dream refers to an actual outing. I took my son and a friend of his to New York to see the Mets (the opera would have been at the Met, too), so there were three tickets. And there was a fourth, which I gave to a friend, hoping he would keep me company on the drive down and back; but it turned out he had to meet us at the

Polo Grounds and go on from there to fly to the Coast. I had also a choice of three combinations of routes by which to get to New York, and was pleased, as in the dream, that there was one of them (by which we in fact returned) I hadn't used for some years, so that it would be unfamiliar to me.

I suppose the tall bald man in the phone booth represents the penis making himself at home in the usual place; subject equally of *Tristan* and *Don Giovanni*. The "three ways" (corresponding to three tickets? for a ticket entitled one to 'get in') is new to my dreams, which have typically expressed interest in two ways, two paths, two of everything. I have referred this trait in my analyses to, first, a nasty notion of anal as equal to vaginal penetration, second, a childhood myth about anal birth (particularly clear in a dream about a month ago, which I was too embarrassed to record, probably because the nasty, muddy road of two roads into town was traveled by a Negro, indicating in addition to everything else a horrifying segregationist tendency to my ucs). Now there are three ways, three tickets, one of which I want to give to a girl I once (with a good many of my classmates) lusted after and speculated a good deal about.

When I put down the names of the operas, an echo in my mind said distinctly: *Fidelio.* I don't know how legitimate(?) it is to include this as part of the material, but it makes three operas giving three distinct alternative ways of regarding love. I have a guilty association to *Fidelio,* too: A friend (one with whom I used to discuss dream symbolism) made me a gift of a recording of this opera, and because I am in an unmusical state of mind this past month I haven't played it yet, but pretended I had when writing to thank him. (These dreams

don't miss a trick, do they? he said with a certain admira-
tion of the technique showing through his chagrin.)

Now this dream occurs in and refers to a period of my life
in several respects critical. I am about to be a father once
again, fully thirteen years after the first time. Toward the
end of my wife's pregnancy I have been unusually listless
about sex, and though her appearance supplies an innocent
reason for my want of interest in her I have characteristically
had the glum thought that I might be getting a bit past it.
And I have been for some time in a (corresponding?) period
of artistic impotence, or paralysis, partly involving the choice
between poetry and fiction (the two ways again!), a condi-
tion which I have been trying to examine in these pages,
which may represent in themselves a 'third way' of writing,
as well as being an attempt to find some third way, probably
combining the linguistic powers of poetry with the archi-
tectural qualities of the novel.

I note here a pretty economy
in the dream representation. The three operas stand for three
ways of love, but also for three quite distinct art styles (and
I remember remarking about *Fidelio* in particular, some
weeks ago, that with Beethoven music becomes political in
an overt way that it is not in Mozart.

No doubt it says
something about my elective affinities both sexual and artistic
that I am quite clear the opera was *Don Giovanni*, though I
repeatedly substituted *Tristan* in saying the dream over,
and later had the curiously insistent echo of *Fidelio* in my
mind as I wrote it down.

The thought crosses my mind that the tall bald man in the
phone booth, whom I have just supplied with spectacles, was
my father. This is perhaps altogether too pious and academic,

the more so as my father has so recently died; but I note an additional item, that Mother sent me, among many of his things, his sun glasses. My father was not bald.

Anyhow, I did not get into the phone booth, I did not get into the opera. Both projects were canceled by my waking up, which was accompanied by a complex of three feelings: lust, fear, and the hopelessness or disgust indicated by my thinking the girl (and myself) too old.

       These three feelings, I am interested and saddened to observe, correspond with considerable precision to those I have had about my relation to literature as I have expressed it in what I have written over the past fortnight or so. I have repeatedly had to speak of my desire to write (opera = work), the fear that consistently balanced this desire, and the resultant of these forces in a certain fastidiousness or disgust (for self and work together) which would constantly make me give up before even beginning. Even the ideas I have had for stories, and written down in the course of this examination, may relate to the three operas, though here the correspondence is by no means exact: but the story about the girl who drowned, even in some phrases such as "castle by the sea in a foreign land," sufficiently alludes to *Tristan.*

The nub of the analysis is a thought I have had for a couple of days and not put down, not wanted to put down. Whether in phantasy or in fact, writing was once supposed to be the highest sort of pleasure; why bother to continue with it if it has become only a dreadfully painful duty? It is quite clear that even the language of this thought (highest sort of pleasure) refers to sexual pleasure quite as much as writing. Is it a duty to continue to demonstrate one's powers, maritally or artistically?

Now the dream tries to say all this with reference to two things, phoning someone, and going to the opera. Leaving the first aside for the moment, "going to the opera" deserves some separate consideration. One goes to the opera, and this is true of opera more than of any other art, either for pleasure or as a duty, to show that one is civilized, up on these things, &c. It is true that I take much less pleasure in music than I used to do, look back on that period of my life—when we first got to know the Mozart operas, for instance—with regret, and have not seldom had the ridiculously puritan notion that I should make myself listen to 'good music' more than I do.

But because *opera* means *works*, going to the opera means also going to work, or doing a work of art. The relation to music, then, expresses this thought about my life as a writer: You are going to the opera, to an opera which will express one of the possible ways you have of being yourself; that is, you are going to work. But you will never get there (never do the work) because this work, which you formerly regarded as a pleasurable expression of power and creative genius, now appears to you only as a mean responsibility grudgingly offered to your 'career,' the idea you have of yourself as a result of having written for pleasure, and which you now unworthily seek to maintain as a hollow show, a matter of public credit (I *am* a writer, he cried). Inescapably, this analysis wishes to apply itself in the sexual realm as well: Like writing, sex used to seem inexhaustibly pleasurable, though with its pleasures much pain was always mixed; now there is a weariness. This weariness is owing in part to your wife's pregnancy, true (you are asked to become a father again, this time after your own father's death), but you do not even entertain in a lively manner daydreams of infidelity with this one and that one while your wife is out of action, during what the Elizabethans called the gander's month.

So much for the opera I never got in to see. The phone booth, the call I never made, is a similar compound representation of sexual and artistic thoughts (wooing the Muse?). While the phone booth is occupied, I am impatient with desire to call —— (a thought intervenes here, for me alone to remember; it is kept back because it involves another person; but it fits, it fits). But as soon as the booth is free I awaken in a conflict of feeling issuing in helplessness. Writing is in some sense speaking to someone, it is also an act of love, or faith; that something is able to be said, that someone will listen, maybe even that the third ticket will be used after all and I shall attend the tragic farce of the great seducer with the Muse beside me. In sleep a king, but waking no such matter.

Supposing the man in the phone booth to have been my father (who turned to an artistic career late in life, with surprising success), the position worsens rapidly. Out of reverence for my death father * (for reverence read: guilt over disobedience, self-punishment, refusal to compete, inability to become a father in my own right) I withdraw from art as from sexuality. Despite my lust and my will to art, I wake up affrighted and in some despair so as not to have to enter the woman, speak with the Muse, attend to the work.

The girl in the dream wrote to me a few years back, with the surprising announcement that she had taken up the profession

* I write 'death father' for 'dead father.' I allow it to stand because I don't understand. Is there then another father, a 'life father,' implied as a shadow though unable to appear in the dream? I have frequently thought of a certain man as my father in the spirit; of two men, in fact, one of them dead. He was tall and bald; the other small, balding, wearing eyeglasses. Both artists.

of bookbinding, and I should call on her if I wanted any fine binding done. Apart from the obvious fact that even 'book-binding,' as coming from this lady, would turn into a sexual expression, this circumstance helps to explain why she, and not some other, appears in the dream; it is as though to say to me, along with the other dream-thoughts: Your interest in literature has become purely external, you no longer want art, all you want is to produce one book after another, as a professional matter; you might marry this particular muse and spend your life binding nonsense (or nothing) in tooled leather. (And 'binding,' in RAF slang, means complaining; which I have been doing a good bit of in this writing, too.)

The sexual, or family, story again harmonizes, by equating "Produce one book after another" with "producing one child after another."

For a man whose conscious mind insists that he wishes above all things to continue to write, whose conscious mind says that he wants a great deal more sex before he dies, whose conscious mind tells him that he is grownup, a father, a success at life despite his many doubts, this is a spectacularly pessimistic dream, amounting even to what one might call a rude awakening. So this, it seems to be saying, is the end. No matter how much you congratulate yourself on having kept in reserve a third, new way of getting to the opera house, you will hear no music. That part of life, with all it represents, is over, and you must put up with it as best you are able, remembering with a little humility, please, that it has happened to better and more gifted human beings than yourself.

What this dream says to me, or what I have made it say to me, is the sorrowfulest and most hopeless of messages. But what I feel about it, as the result of having written these words, is a sort of power. As though I had first looked over the edge and seen the nothing that is there. But I did look, and said what I was able to.

One small crumb of comfort. Kierkegaard, under one of his pseudonyms (Johannes de Silentio? Victor Eremita?) says something to this effect: The greatest achievement of genius is sleep. I know I am quoting it wrong, and probably misremember its source as well, but something tells me he says this in *Either/Or*. *Either/Or*, you remember, is about *Don Giovanni*.

I don't know if I dare look that up. But probably I will, for even confronting things is likely to be habit-forming.

The question I especially want to go on with, since I gave it no more than the most cursory and received notation earlier, is whether in fact writing was always so pleasurable a business as I make out toward the bottom of page two above. Also the related question, whether writing and sexual experience are analogies one of the other (if somehow sexual experience is the 'secret meaning' of writing referred to some days ago and immediately abandoned, or suppressed). The connexion is certainly made—the two are given as alternatives—in some beautiful lines of *Lycidas*, which now I think of it I have been mumbling more or less accurately, and without much thought of their meaning or application to me, for several days preceding the dream:

> Alas! what boots it with uncessant care
> To tend the homely slighted Shepherds trade,
> And strictly meditate the thankless Muse,
> Were it not better don as others use,

To sport with *Amaryllis* in the shade,
Or with the tangles of *Neæra's* hair?
Fame is the spur
&c.

My earliest recollection of what was a big work at least for
a schoolboy of eighteen is that it was immensely difficult,
and accompanied by much misery and agony of self-doubt,
recrimination, the vicious circle in which an hour wasted re-
quires by some mystical logic the waste of another hour,
and so on. Probably I was occupied with the thoughts behind
those seventy pages or so for a matter of four months. But
it is also probable (that is, a memory I am not very certain
of) that the actual composition took place in an explosion of
energy and clarity which was (by the writer's perhaps curious
definition of pleasure) pleasurable extremely. At least such
a mode of composition checks with many subsequent ex-
periences. There have come times in my life when for as long
as was necessary doubt, which did not altogether go away,
lost all its effective force, and I learned to recognize myself
as that kind of writer who must unsparingly devote himself
during that brief interval. My first novel took me three years,
because I worked only during the summers. Even so, its crisis
and completion, a matter of some sixty pages done almost
continuously, in two sessions of maybe fifteen hours each, was
preceded by (a) a mean quarrel with a friend, and (b) a month
during which I did nothing but (of all things) play golf. My
second novel followed only after five years of what I may as
well call miscarriages (and after the burning of most or all
of these, amounting to several hundreds of pages); I did it in
just under two months, during a summer by the sea. My third
I began toward the end of one school term, writing a couple
of chapters; I finished the rest, during the subsequent vaca-
tion, in just twenty-eight days: about two hundred pages.

On a smaller scale, with essays and reviews, my experience has been similar. Even doing very compassable jobs, there would be first much perplexity, lasting many days, a sense that the object was an impossible one, a fumbling around for the handle of the subject (like finding an end before you can unravel a ball of string); then one day it would go with speed and ease and delight.

In writing poetry, though, it was always very different; the element of pleasure was always dominant over this experience, I never wanted to leave the desk before I was finished with at least a complete draft. I have usually thought this was so because, in poetry, I never knew what I wanted to write before it began to appear; the line, the cadence, the formal problem, always or almost always preceded anything that might be called 'the idea.' It is part of the delight in poetry, too, that there *are* formal problems; going at these relieves you of a certain pretentiousness connected with what you are supposed to be saying; you let it say itself, if only because you are so blessedly busy getting things to fit.

So it appears that for me to say I formerly thought of writing as an exalted pleasure is a theoretical, or mythical remark; it has a heroic pathos, but when closely inspected turns out to be true and not true at the same time, or true in some ways and untrue in others.

This also: After so much time and labor expended in blaming yourself, be so fair as for a moment to acknowledge the immense difficulty in the object proposed. Imaginative composition may be the hardest sort of work anywhere in the world, and I mean this in a fairly prosy, not hyperbolical way. For in every other sort of work an object exists in view, which the work is designed to accomplish; but in writing a fiction this object cannot clearly be brought into view except by the very work designed to accomplish it—a definition in which the little word 'it' becomes supremely problematic: How can you know *it*, or even that there is (could be) an *it* to be known, until you have said what this *it* is? And how can you say what it is, except by making *it*?

A dream last night after writing the foregoing pages of analysis. This document or whatever you call it I am engaged in writing has now become supremely important. I give M one copy to take to the bank vault, and I keep the other. But somehow it turns out I have taken the other copy downstairs to the living room, where M is keeping the first copy until she can get it to the bank. This is foolish, because now if there were a fire both copies would be lost. In one further image, M puts a copy in a secret cabinet in the stove.

                If the ms. is put in the stove, it is brought into relation with fire; surely it is the last way a waking person would think of saving something from fire. But in the dream I distinctly thought it a clever solution: Even if the stove should burn up or explode, I said, the ms. will be saved because it is completely enclosed in metal.

                A curious or paradoxical relation of saving and losing here, piously Christian, even. As in a line of Eliot's, "to be redeemed from fire by fire."

Which reminds me that the lines I quoted from *Lycidas* are even more closely related to my thoughts than I saw last night, for they connect not only sex and writing, but sex and writing and drowning, which brings them into line with the story I have been contemplating.

A *copy* is perfectly traditional for a *child*. The copy put for safekeeping into a drawer in the stove is a wry representation of the mysteries of sexual generation. The image probably came to mind from my having read, a few days ago, in a compilation of medieval texts, a *Lesson in Anatomy* from a sermon by Berthold (birth + old or hold!) of Ratisbon, or Regensburg, in which the stomach is described several times as "like a cauldron on the fire," and suchlike.

The analysis becomes speculative here, but it is hard not to see again a choice of two ways represented by the bank vault and the stove. The first is the way of death, for it speaks to me of my father's body, laid up not in a grave but in the family *vault*. The vault is where you keep money, securities, dead things. The relation of money with shit is perfectly appropriate if I recall that the 'two ways' so often occurring in my dreams have to do with the choice between anus and vagina. So if I took a copy of my ms. to the bank vault for safekeeping, that would be as much as to say it was over and done with, that it belonged to death and waste, that I had got it out of me (put it behind me), but that it could no longer affect the future (except, maybe, destructively). Whereas the copy stored in the stove *is* the future, the unborn child put in the place of fire (sexual passion, urine) which is paradoxically the safe place and the place of growth.

I note that this dream comes to me in the present tense, and refers though fearfully to the future; whereas yesterday's occurred as though naturally in the past.

"Downstairs to the living room." Whereas in fact both copies are up here in the study, though the daytime self is less concerned about fire than the other. It is possible to read this situation a little further, for it expresses both a wish and a fear. The wish is that my mental life should enter more fully into the life of the family (the living room), but this brings up the fear that when it happens all will be lost (both copies). And the preceding analysis discloses the further thought, distinctly double in nature, about somehow bringing to life (the living room) both dead father and unborn child, also a dangerous business ("if there were a fire both copies would be lost"). Nor is there wanting the hidden significance to warn me that my father cannot be safely put away (the bank vault) except by somehow being brought back to life (the living room).

The relation of upstairs and downstairs seems to say something about the desirability (and danger) of an art which shall be more visceral, say, and less exclusively cerebral, or *civilized*; something my critics have often said, though some with more generosity than others.

So the dream once again responds with considerable compositional wit to my several preoccupations, rebuking me for being a bad son and a bad father, needling me just where it hurts, with a threat to the artistic life which has become "supremely important" in so vulnerable and vain a sense that I now think in terms of preserving past achievement (the bank vault) as much as of abandoning that false security in order to move ahead in my art.

Now the dream, whenever you are for some reason able to read it, turns out to be a supremely novelistic (or poetic, or dramatic) imagining, unfolding from its apparently surrealist or absurd outward surface a richness of ordered and relevant content. Surely all this is trying to tell me something I want to know?

The dream is in this respect anyhow like a story, for all stories are ridiculous when abstracted from the art which gives them life; that is why abstracts of the Greek myths are so appallingly confused and confusing and a bore (a story does not admit, or admits only within the narrowest limits, of our saying, Well, it was either this way or it was that way, or, some say, quite different from either); and the same is true of the plot of *Hamlet* if you tell it independently of *Hamlet*. While working on novel or story, I have had to hold myself to it on one day after another by saying, Yes, I know it is stupid, I know it couldn't have happened—but go on with it anyhow.

Very often I have dreams which I cannot understand, even though I may take a superficial pleasure in their picturesque qualities. Perhaps it is that the same resistances which keep me from understanding certain dreams, or dreams at certain times during my life, keep me from writing certain of my stories, or any story at certain times.

And I note again, as I noted yesterday, that the disagreeable content and tendency of the dream does not diminish, and may even increase, a sense of pleasurable power at being able to see deeply into it and say what I see. This circumstance relates to what I have sometimes said of the essential of art: that the greatness of the human voice, and its nobility, and its poignance, are most fully heard when it speaks of disaster, hopelessness, failure unredeemable. . . . See, my women, The crown of the earth doth melt.

Of course, all oracles are ambiguous, and the perfect dream, the perfect story, would be perfectly dialectical, shining with "the light of hope out of the utmost hopelessness." Despite its monitory aspect, this dream also says to me: Fear neither death nor birth, and do not fear the fire of passion which seems to destroy, for it is the agent of alchemical change:

You give yourself away into the woman, or the work, to make the future grow strange and new.

The art of storytelling seems to imitate, not always very expertly, the art of dreaming. To both, interpretation is necessary, whether it be so simple as the moralizing of the *Gesta Romanorum*, so pedantically strict as the fourfold method of medieval times, or so complex, ambivalent, and reflexive as the construction of fugue or canon, the associative investigations of psychoanalysis, or the patterns of initiation as applied, for instance, to *The Tempest* by Colin Still.

But there's more to it than that. Nebuchadnezzar's therapists would have been perfectly able to interpret the dream, if he had told them what it was. But he wisely or stubbornly insisted that they had to tell him what he had dreamed first.

Now I have, at certain times anyhow, some skill at the interpretation business. I very much doubt it is psychoanalytic skill, or that it will tell me very much about my nature, except maybe about my fictional nature as a writer (I become one of a very small gallery of character types). For this skill of mine, such as it is, comes from reading poems, and the pleasure in demonstrating the power of compositional integrity, in dream or poem or play or novel, outweighs for me the disagreeableness of the revelations made therein. So I am still, it seems clear, a theoretical sort of human being rather than a real one. The beast that does not exist.

A story, perhaps, is theoretically made the other way round: as if Nebuchadnezzar had told his people the analysis, and required them to do what they were professionally qualified to do, reconstruct the dream. Theoretically, I say, because of course it doesn't seem to happen that way. A story comes to you for the telling, and you either are or are not able to tell it. When you have told a good many stories in your time, you may come to some understanding of how it is that a new story which attracts you is the old story in a new disguise; or you may see at the least that you possess, or are possessed by, certain constants of imagery (how the preoccupation with drowning is visible in two or three of my stories and several poems) or of situation (Shakespeare and his characteristic relation of two brothers).

"Real life" seldom, yet sometimes, reveals itself as having the interpretable depth of a dream. We suspect this quality to be an intermittence of our vision, however, rather than something existing "out there." When "real life" thus shows itself, gaining a certain transpicuousness even while keeping its weight and solid specificity, it becomes artistic, fateful, or subject to art. Here is an instance, though repugnant to me to have to record, of how something like this happened.

When my father was ill, and it was beginning to be apparent that he was going to die, I came to visit him, then went on a journey of a few days before coming back to see him again; during this interval I came out with a severe cold and cough. My phantasy on this was somewhat as follows: Now I have an excuse not to visit my father, for if he were to catch cold in addition to his present illness he would certainly die. And I imagined myself making this excuse on the phone to my mother, imagining her response: Of course you mustn't come, how very sensible you were to phone, &c. But because I was so near New York I couldn't make myself do that. Finally, as a compromise, I paid the visit, stood in the door for a couple of minutes while I explained the situation, and left with full parental approval.

This cold, I conceive, displayed very fully the dramaturgic powers of the ucs. So far as I am able to see, it served the following real and phantastic purposes. It much shortened a visit I resisted making, out of selfishness and fear. I could make this visit, so to say, in a purely formal sense, without content or intimacy. At the same time, my parents could not possibly disapprove of my behavior, and even had to praise it. The cold and cough, which were really rather alarming, and accompanied by a fever of 102, put me absurdly into competition with my father, saying: Look here, I am sick too, you are not the only one deserving of sympathy. This illness also represented my hostility to my father by threatening to kill him, which the cold gave me power to do.

Finally, by one superb turn of dramatic cruelty, the cold was my revenge on my father, whom I punished by not kissing him. For in childhood, whenever my father was seriously angry at me the first symptom of it would be his saying, in a voice I learned to recognize quite well, when he came to breakfast, "Don't kiss me, I have a cold." On such occasions I would then have to wait the whole day, until he came home, under the threat of his powerful, unforgiving will.

So this cold of mine was an immense dramatic achievement, concentrating into symptomatic and evidential form the substance of my feelings for my father, my timidity about sickness and death, my longing for unearned approval, and so on, including even the selection of an illness which parodied his (pains in the chest, coughing) and one whose name, *cold*, characterized publicly, yet in seeming innocence the coldness of the heart.

It even brought tears to my eyes. I had defensively determined, in the event one of my relatives should bring attention to my not crying, to say rather sternly, "He brought me up not to cry, he told me men did not cry," &c. But I was relieved that this ridiculous (though for that matter not false) expedient did not turn out to be necessary.

I am a little shaken, less by having had to record this example than by observing to what a degree I continued while doing so in the same 'cold' artistic fascination with the multivalent reach of the anecdote that I felt in the interpreting of the dreams.

      As though to say: Yes, I am a loathsome fellow, but beautifully composed!

And all through these so intimate, so personal, observations runs the thought that I shall one day publish them, in a gesture of confessional defiance or proud self-contempt. For I am trying to tell the truth, and it is a trouble to me.

To write, then, is to say, whether pleading or in accusation, I am not the only one. You others, you too . . . and wait to hear the silence echoing through the world.

23 VII

A man who has always prided himself on being 'civilized,' and regards life as an 'art,' finds that his life is turning into an art work. This is horrifying to him when he understands it, for of course an art work has an end, and its major purpose is to reach that end. Nothing happens at random any more, the world gains a great, a fatal, significance.

But this is only what happens whenever you try to *say* what happens; you prehend the world by means of artistic conventions and figurations not prior, perhaps, to all experience, but certainly prior to the one you are trying to relate.

I try to think about memory. Almost nothing happens. As a subject, memory is empty of content and impossible to be thought: While I try to think about it, I am unable even to remember anything. It is even extraordinarily difficult to remember one particular instant, day, or sequence of happenings, for the mind won't focus.

The day I broke my foot. Which foot? The right one, I see myself coming down hard on its outer edge, hearing a loud snap which seemed at the moment to have nothing to do with me. I was able to walk for a few minutes after that, then the pain began. I sat down and waited on the field, while F went to get his car. I remember that he took me to the doctor's house, but this is a purely intellectual and as it were abstract memory; that is, I have no physical impression of the ride in the car. The doctor was out, and F took me home. Later the doctor showed up. Somehow, I was well enough, even without a cast, to go to F's house for supper that evening; that was the day F's dog was run over and killed. That was nine years ago. I have 'memory' but no image, no detail; on this episode the memory works like a catalogue.

Having typhoid. Thirty years ago. Remember playing tennis (the foot, too, was broken on the tennis court), having a headache, was playing with H, a fat boy, no memory of his face, how I got home and to bed. That was in early September (must have been) between camp and school. I was in bed at least through November. Had a nurse who taught me dirty songs (not remembered, text or tune). I am said to have been some time in delirium: no recollection. Convalescence: breaking out in red spots, which the doctor circled in blue ink; his fountain pen was green. Ate a great deal, mostly steak, during convalescence. The bed in my room a brown, square-cut couch; I used to pretend I was in a kayak while going to sleep. Later, being taken to a heart specialist who did a cardiograph (no details, this memory overlaid by a later electroencephalograph done in the RCAF). He told me I could not play football. I must have been, I know I was, aggrieved, but there is no tone to this recollection. Being taken by Mother to the new school: A row of green lockers survives, nothing more.

It is as though I had already lost my life.

This morning I watched some reddish-brown ants crossing the path, foraging in the grass on one side and bringing home to the other side identical-looking mouthfuls of some white stuff. Myself, I brought home two seeding plants, one a puffball cosmic affair of what resembled small spider webs mounted spherically on spikes of yellow, the other a compact white fluff that felt like cat's fur. I learned the name of the blue damselfly: Agrion; and that of course when they fly together it is not copulation. The real reason is charming: They are very weak-legged, and when the female goes underwater to oviposit she finds it difficult to climb back through the surface tension. So they make a funny marital arrangement, wherein she pushes him up through the water top and then he flies her out. How very gay!

And of course I remember a great deal more about this morning. So, only a little surprisingly, it seems that the more or less immediate past occurs not only in greater detail but also with much more feeling, trivial as the events of it are, than crises of my life which are at a greater distance in time. Is this always true? Is it necessarily true? Perhaps not always and not necessarily. Quite early in childhood there was a portable phonograph, a black leather or leatherette box you wound by hand; the turntable was made of three beautiful silver arms that folded in for carrying and you unfolded them flat for playing. I used to play "Ramona" over and over again. That makes me remember two other favorites: "Constantinople," "Valencia." Those silver arms were so neat!

There is one kind of memory that arranges things chronologically, a kind of *curriculum vitae* uninterested in feeling and detail; there is another kind that brings up isolated brilliants. These latter do not, however, always remain isolated: I could not have predicted, a moment before, that I would suddenly find two more old songs than I had remembered remembering. (I know Proust has done all this, but I want my life, not Proust's.)

The scar on my sister's face. Did she really get that in our struggle for a doll that broke in our hands? I believe so, but this belief is not a memory, or it is a memory of having been told so. The portrait of us in oils, on a red settee, wherein the artist's difficulty with perspective made us appear to have shoed stumps instead of feet. No memory at all of sitting for this.

We played football in the living room, and the ball left the marks of its nose and seam on the ceiling so that we got found out. One Christmas morning we came into the living room secretly and managed to knock the tree over—did we put it back on its feet?

Notice that these three memories have somehow grouped themselves about feet, even using metaphor to do so in the last instances. I did not predict their appearance, I was writing with the first and simplest phrases to come into my head; I suppose though that the use of 'feet' in one sentence has a more than stylistic bearing on its appearance in the next two. Just as one memory of a disaster on a tennis court was succeeded by another disaster also connected with a tennis court.

Electric trains, a green engine and an orange engine. Christmas probably brought that up.

By contrast, if you were imagining a childhood in a novel, how much marvelous and 'vivid' detail you would be sure to get in. If, that is, you were a certain sort of novelist, which I am not. But it wouldn't even be hard to do.

Those three memories were linked by the living room (where that portrait hung) as well as by feet; and they brought up another a few minutes ago, in which I used to go into the living room very early in the morning and steal candy, which

I took back to my room and ate in what I hoped was secrecy but rarely was. Where, by the way, has candy gone? It used to be the staff of life, for years I ate far too much of it (and aggravated my eczema). I suppose it has been replaced by smoking, mostly.

So a first memory, in any given attempt, may be arbitrary. But its connections with the memories which succeed it look quite plain, and there may be several of them: The ones just told are related by 'feet,' by 'living room,' by stealth and early morning. Or, rather, they are so related except for the portrait: But if the portrait, which began the cluster, is connected to the others by the obvious means of feet and living room, probably I should infer further that it is connected to the others also by stealth, early morning, and guilt; perhaps it was looking at that likeness of myself, seeing myself as a stranger, a mystery, that represented the secret beginnings of art, that mystery which brings me now to search the self in a spirit of guilt and isolation and some secrecy. Or else there is some meaningful episode belonging to the portrait, which I am unable to bring back because it represents something I can't look at.

The morning of the birth of my sister (but which one, and was I three or eight?). This is not arbitrary either, for it was early morning, a good deal of stealthy coming and going in the house, no one telling me anything; I felt neglected.

24 VII

The word 'memory' goes back to 'mindful' (L. *memor*), clearly in the sense also of 'worried' or 'careful.' For it is said to be akin to the Greek for 'anxiety' (*mermoros*, anxious) and 'witness' (*martys*).

Aristotle: "The most skillful interpreter of dreams is he who has the faculty of observing resemblances."

A bold and silly speculation: If we had no memory we could not die. More prosily: Death would have a different and less painful sense.

The memory of pain is not painful, of pleasure not pleasurable. The memory of embarrassment is embarrassing, though, and the memory of humiliation humiliating. The connexion with anxiety is again clear.

For example: The dentist, several years ago, passed under my nose a piece of the nerve of one of my teeth: quite the most awful stench in my experience, and it came straight out of me. But I say this now without any affect, any physical feeling of awfulness, because, I suppose, no guilty symbolism ever attached itself to this pain. But I can still, over a lapse of a great many years, flinch at the remembrance of occasions on which I behaved badly, was rude, arrogant, drunk, or else cowardly and inadequate to a situation.

I seem to be saying, Freud somewhat to the contrary, that we do not by any means invariably suppress what is disagreeable, certainly not to the point of forgetting it. In fact, the extreme form of what I am getting at would claim that memory is most sharply related to guilt.

Now what became of the girl and boy in that portrait? I can to a certain extent, and no doubt with many inaccuracies, see it now. They sit together on the red settee, she in a white dress on the spectator's left, he—wearing what?—with his hair, still blond at that time, on the right. His hair is brushed back in a pompadour, style then fashionable. She has long ringlets of brown hair at her ears. She has white pumps, he black patent leather ones (very badly painted, as beforesaid), they button over white stockings. Her expression is an indescribable compound of sullen and shy, his is bolder, perhaps a trifle insolent, perhaps somewhat defensive. No smiles.

It now comes to me that a poem I wrote about ten years ago, called "An Old Picture," made a distorted allusion to this portrait without my ever suspecting it; I represented, anyhow, "Two children, dressed in court costume," and the anecdote of the poem stressed the helplessness of these children under the traditional impositions of scepter and book, their fates already arranged by the parents (in the poem, the bishop, the queen). The poem ends with some considerable bitterness toward these grownups:

> These hold the future tightly reined,
> It shall be as they have ordained:
> The bridal bed already made,
> The crypt also richly arrayed.

A dream of many years ago. Two women, fairly young, in something like what might have been special motoring costume for the twenties. They stand on the steps of a grey stone house, under a porte-cochere, and a voice outside this picture said: They do not know that they were both killed in an accident the same afternoon.

I do not know when I dreamed, or thought of, that; it connects itself with a vague memory that my mother used to drive a car when I was very young, but later gave it up (a summer house in Far Rockaway? the one where the portable phonograph was?), but the image of the two women, and what the voice said of them, has long been to me an emblem of the mystery and terror of time. I don't know why I suddenly recollected it again while thinking of the portrait of my sister and myself, and of the two children in the poem (who are supposed, evidently, to be betrothed royalties).

But though I don't know in particular, I can see that the poem blames adults for the children's future, and that the dream might be taken as expressing hostility to one of the women in the photograph (for the memory makes it appear that they were in a photograph) who may be my mother.

The expression in the poem, "tightly reined," with its allusion to control under the figure of driving, may have been responsible for the rising of that memory; when I put down those two words, at least, I had a sight of the strap of one of my black pumps in the portrait (rein = strap).

A passing impression while waking up this morning: if I were telling the story of those children I would name the painter of the portrait Mr. Dappertutto (*Tales of Hoffman,* from which I remember only the mysterious beginning of the baritone air, *"Tourne, miroir,"* with another bit about *diamant* and *scintille*). 'Dapper' has to do with those patent leather pumps, and the name as a whole cryptically alludes to a situation in which "everything is open."

(Cf. with reference to the first of the two recent dreams, *Don Giovanni: "e aperto a tutti, a tutti quanti,"* inviting the people into his ballroom. Also, in connection with ———'s being a bookbinder, what Leporello says of Elvira: *"para un libro stampato!"* where I took the adjective for a long time to mean 'bound,' and with the title *stamped* on it, before learning it meant 'printed.')

In the portrait I could not have been more than seven (and my sister four). But several associations want to refer to a later time. The pumps, for instance, speak of dancing, and of that dreadful dancing school I was sent to, maybe about age twelve; and Dappertutto's Air (I see for a moment the blue label of the black record, I watch its mysterious circling) must be associated with a time no earlier than my thirteenth or fourteenth year, when I wanted to be an operatic tenor and was only gradually coming to understand it would have to be a basso if anything.

              Perhaps that situation, in which through no fault of my own but through the physiological process of growing up I had to abandon the heroic roles for those of the villain, counselor, commenter on the action, and maybe buffoon, formed the early model for the position I most often take with respect to writing, favoring an ironic clarity and depth of tone to the unreserved lyric bursting forth.

A little, a very little, sexual experimentation with my sister must probably date to about this time; but that is not a new memory, and was never in fact really forgotten. It is possible, however, that this memory merely covers something of the sort that happened much earlier, at the time of the portrait.

Something I remember being told in childhood: My mother pretends, for a home movie, to make love to another man. I threaten to kill him.

The connexion, again, is *picture*. We have the portrait, the poem about a portrait, the photograph of the two women in the dream, or daydream, and now this home movie. My vocation as a grownup has to do with making images, but I have never much cared for photographs. The same sister is a professional phototgrapher, whose pictures are spectacular, shocking, dramatic, and concentrate on subjects perverse and queer (freaks, professional transvestites, strong men, tattooed men, the children of the very rich). Thou shalt make no graven image. Unlike a great many people, I do not keep pictorial representations of my family on the walls, on the desk, in the wallet (but this does not seem to be a strong prohibition; just now a photograph of my son at about the age of seven, done by the same sister, is tacked to my bulletin board next to a photograph of Willie Mays given me by my son). I was always, well into so-called adult life, embarrassed by a photograph of myself on my father's desk; one's photographed face appears to me singularly vulnerable and without defense.

So the portrait has reached out to draw to itself a cluster of notions relating to visual imagery, representation, likeness. Here are some associated reflexions.

E. H. Gombrich, writing about the magical origin and nature of representation, says something striking to this effect: Though we do not generally regard ourselves as living by the equations of magic between a person and his image, we should still feel shocked by someone who, for example, took a photograph of a friend and ran a pin into its eyes.

I have frequently felt accused by the eyes of portraits, because their very aimlessness confers on them the power of following you around the room.

I once sent a girl a photograph of a boy peeing. About age eleven, or maybe twelve, we all were.

People, tourists, say, who habitually respond to a sight by photographing it, appear to me very defensive about life. As though they wished to kill reality in order to guarantee it, as though only the two-dimensional past were to have a real (a historical) existence. They are ever-present witnesses to the character of civilization as mediate, abstract, in a sense *memorized*; the living memory delegated to that 'objective' one in the black box. (The portable phonograph too was a black box, standing in a similar relation to experience.) Poetry is a struggle against this kind of imagery, and I recall characterizing a certain kind of bad poem as "a twelve-line image with a two-line caption telling you what to think." Much later, I made this into a distinction (in conversation with the same sister), saying that I had been twenty years in the poetry business without, so far as I can say, telling people what they ought to think; good art tells you only what you do in fact think.

Photography, considered now not as an art but only as a widespread human activity, paradoxically stresses seeing at the expense of seeing. It works, does it, as a kind of guarantee of a past existence? Implicit in the guarantee is security: The existence is safely past, reduced to a flat surface, color removed, and so on. To be echt analytic, it imitates looking through the keyhole at mother and father, but it takes the curse off this, as well as punishing for the presumption of looking at all, by reducing the observed experience to a flat statement: I was there. It also pretends that what the camera fiend(!) saw was no dread secret but, after all, only the Eiffel Tower. It implies also that to look at life without the interposition of this mysterious amulet (bound in skin, worn round the neck, incised with cryptic symbolism referring to light) would be somewhat dangerous.

Metaphorical corollaries: the film (veil?) is *exposed*, it is *developed*. It would be ruined by being *prematurely exposed*.

"Mirate la dottrina che s'asconde sotto il *velame* degli versi strani."

Hence perhaps the famous phrase of reassurance: The camera cannot lie. Whereas that statement is the camera's initial lie. Another such phrase: One picture is worth a thousand words. The camera, interested in surfaces, grew with a materialist civilization interested in "simple location in time and space" (Whitehead), and makes the constant claim that reality is visible. Language, on the contrary, constantly asserts reality to be secret, invisible, a product of relations rather than things. The camera, whether in the hands of reporter or scientist or detective, pries into secrets, wants everything *exposed* and *developed* (in an interesting recent phrase, we now 'develop' information, that is, information of a discreditable character). The camera wants to *know*. But if my hypothesis is correct, this knowledge is dialectically determined to be unsatisfying, so that there can be no end to the taking of pictures (this common phrase also now reveals a metaphorical content, where taking = stealing). Everything known becomes an object, unsatisfactory (not what you really wanted to know), hence to be treated with contempt and forgotten in the illusory thrill of taking the next picture.

In a recent poem on this subject, using some of these metaphorical materials but not going so far as to involve the primal scene, I gave three examples of what the tourists photographed: the Vatican, the Sphinx, and, in the Badlands, the nostrils of the Fathers. All associated with power, authority, mystery, the parents.*

Memory: a photograph of Mother and Father standing before the great Buddha at Kamakura. Some elusive thought about this had to do with their looking quite young, innocent, American, smiling (contrast the smile of the Buddha); how in spite of all their travels (from Hilton to Hilton ride the mad pilgrims) they remained toward the end of life much as one imagined them at the beginning, innocently excited by the world. †

Marvelous how very clever one can be when it's a question of turning the discussion away from one's own secrets.

But it is very pleain (and note that spelling, which pleads and is plain) that the brilliant critique of photography (my sister's art) is quietly but quite specifically intended to be set against writing (my art) as guilt against innocence. The statement, for example, that "language constantly asserts reality to be secret,

---

* All subjects to be looked *up* to even physically, as though one were a child looking at a grownup; which is I suppose our real relation with heroic monuments anyhow. And it is a little remarkable that tourists with cameras are so frequently found enacting this relation by focusing on subjects that tower high over them (as at Rockefeller Center).

† That too may be one of the camera's inept falsehoods; I could see them equally well as somewhat indifferent to the world, and as experiencing only the narrowest range of what it has to offer, and that always the same.

invisible, a product of relations rather than things," may be aesthetically very intelligent, but is noteworthy on less attractive grounds as well. That is, by identifying myself with language, as against photography, I covertly seek to exculpate myself from any charge of having spied on the parents; their doings are still "secret, invisible." And the metaphors in the phrase apposed: "relations," yes, but not "things," o no, never "things." The whole phrase might be translated: Children (product) are really (in reality) brought into this world by marriage, or families (relations), but not by genitals (things).

A memory of *hearing* * my parents behind closed doors and being terribly shocked, but this was a quarrel. Or at least that's what I say now. Possibly a screen memory. In later life, but still early adolescence, my aunt, who collected art objects, showed me some Syrian statuettes of men and women. O, they're fighting, I said. Look again, dear, said she. This aunt is also supposed to have told my sister (who told me) that Mother was pregnant with me before marriage.

In early life, my sister and I used to blame one another, get one another punished, quite a lot. The above analysis, no matter how much I might insist that I was specifically excepting my sister as an artist from my remarks about photography, may well be another such attempt.

The Syrian statuettes are another item in the representation cluster, here specifically the representation of the forbidden. By now, I would expect the source of my difficulties in writing about sex and love, my distaste for putting down the physical details *in fiction*, to be located, if it ever is, in some experience

---

* My imagination is dominantly aural, and poetry for me is not primarily 'imagery' but a sequence of sounds which with their meanings form the miraculous equivalent of something existing in nature.

having to do with a picture, a statue, a photograph, in which art and sex are related. Note that art-photographs is euphemistic for feelthy pictures.

Rodin's "Le Baiser" reproduced in bronze on the edge of a jade ashtray in the living room.

25 VII

Dreams. 1. A list of titles of home movies, of which I remember only a few scattered words: ruby, spy, secret, spider. Vague association of "a Negro neighborhood."

2. I am at an airport. We take off, and though I am a passenger I can see ahead, and have a sort of telephone receiver at hand through which I am able to hear the pilot; he is saying we are late. We arrive at another airport; instead of a bus there is a truck, and it is crowded. Also hard to get into because so high off the ground. But I find a stirrup on one side and climb up; the pilot approves. Before this, on the way out of the terminal, I farted, but the fart became shit and dropped down my trouser leg to the ground, whereon I reflected comfortably that I would not stink much and therefore need not be embarrassed.

3. A list of ice-cream flavors and amounts and prices, apparently issued to a child or to children, saying how much allowed for individual consumption, for two, for parties.

The man I wrote of a couple of days ago, who found his life turning into an art work, is myself, and the notion is a phantasy about this self-examination; that is, I was taking pleasure in the idea that it might be interminable, but was already being compelled to understand the consequences: that inevitably I should actually make some discoveries about myself, that these would give this writing a species of form, that this developing form would dictate one day a conclusion . . . . and with four dots I leave that sentence endless.

Dreams this morning seem impenetrable. I observe that I very much wanted to leave out the last detail in dream 2 (shit, in childhood, by the way, was known as Number Two), so that I forgot it until after its proper place in the narrative; also I put it in the past tense as though to emphasize its distance from me (putting it *behind* me?). But as soon as I wrote it down the memory became silly rather than sinister. Maybe for some people writing has quite often this function of reducing the magical power of the word to nothing, to a joke? For surely the word 'fart,' in my childhood, was more shameful, and if possible more forbidden, than all the other words (nothing one ever put to the test with a grownup around, though). Even now, though 'fuck' and 'shit' have become permissible, and even rather popular, one much more rarely hears the word 'fart'—except around my house, where because of my son's fascination with this phenomenon we have grown perfectly accustomed to using the word without embarrassment. So part of my embarrassment about writing down the dream episode has another reference, and the first one I think of is this: What I am writing now is private, or even secret. But I have the idea of it as one day being published as a book. So I resist writing details that will get in the way of its being published.

A further thought. To "shit oneself" (childhood expression) was always a shameful thing, something one tried to conceal on those unfortunate occasions when it helplessly happened.

In the dream episode it happens to me when I am a grownup, and seems to say that in this respect I am a mere child again, or still. And the "purely spiritual" fart surprises me by turning into purely material shit; I can't help viewing this as an emblem of this writing itself, which began with the contemplation of imaginative fiction and turned into the exploration of my own more or less real life. Yet the incident has a reassuring termination: The accident, instead of fouling me up, passes away and is left behind.

Dreams 1 and 3 have in common the being about lists (home movies, of course, came from the memory of one related yesterday). Dream 2 seems to stand apart as an exception. Dreams 1 and 3 perhaps imitate what I have been doing recently in writing of memory, that is, make lists of items belonging in a single category, analyzing these items by means of their inter-references with one another, much as if you were to isolate 'the meaning' of a word by noting what was common to a number of usages of it.

Ruby, spy, secret, spider. In connexion with the associated "Negro neighborhood," Ruby is a stereotyped Negro name. Conrad Aiken wrote a poem, "Blues for Ruby Matrix," where the surname brings in the idea of Mother again. "Who can find a virtuous woman? for her price is above rubies." (Proverbs 31:10.) So this part of the dream somehow relates to the home movie in which Mother made love to another man, and the associations seem to protest that she wouldn't do that (one notes, however, that in the proverb a virtuous woman does have a price, though it is rather high).

Spy may relate to yesterday's thoughts about seeing, as may secret. Spider, again, contains spy, though it comes up perhaps because I was reading about spiders the other day, about their web-building technique.

"Dreams this morning seem impenetrable." They still do. But I observe that whatever I have been able to say has come less from the dream than from the criticism of my method in narrating it. This has to do, once again, with fiction, the original subject of these notes. The statement that dreams seem impenetrable relates to the statement in Dream 2: "hard to get into."

I remembered on waking this morning something I said about the age of ten, in a crowded bus full of children, to the effect that girls did have penis and scrotum too, but kept these in a "streamlined case." I had hoped for laughter and approval from this remark, and made it several times, but to no effect, for the others were talking about something else. I was also impressed with the daring of this speculation, for I was generally rather priggishly clean of speech, even though (evidently) containing the complete cesspool of thoughts in silence. The bus in this memory relates to the truck (instead of bus) in the airport dream, and "streamlined case" is from flying, which was my passion for many years dating from Lindbergh's Atlantic flight when I was seven.

Still, these associations seem to me rather random and remote; they are still such as diverge from the dream(s) rather than converging upon the meaning.

"Hard to get into because so high off the ground." In a dream about flying, even if it is said in relation to a truck, these words must have to do with the airplane I flew during the war, which they describe accurately; one entered and left it through a hatch in the belly, and the door, which swung down to permit this, had a stirrup-like step. Even then, I thought of getting out of the airplane, after a mission, as being born.

I left off yesterday upon arriving at the new memory of Rodin's "Le Baiser," with its naked couple embraced upon the edge of a flat dishlike ashtray of jade. All this reminds me of at the moment is perhaps merely picturesque: another statue on the edge of an ashtray was an elephant. In the hall, opposite the elevator door, stood for many years the large bronze of a panther struggling with a python: relation once again of sex with fighting, but how did the elephant interpose himself? That windowless elevator hall has always stood for something very sinister, with its closed doors on two sides, its closed sliding door on the third. It represented a final loneliness (waiting for the elevator on the way to school?).

The smell of the living room early in the morning, after my parents had entertained: cold ashes, sticky chocolates, sweet of soft drinks, still, cold smoke; all in a deep twilight, for the drapes were drawn over the windows.

The first principle of this writing is that everything is relevant; accidents turn up and later, under close reading, prove their right to be here by getting themselves woven into the fabric. The meaning? Well, it may never have a meaning. But the design is constantly making itself over as it draws new materials into its ambit, under its spell. This is a technique, I think, of fiction, or poetry, or magic, more than specifically of psychoanalysis. An exploration into the unknown, which yet shows a tendency to complete itself daily, tendency to form. Perhaps the variation form which I so much favor in poetry and in music, where each step has its own completion yet remains a stage on some larger way. The method owes much to psychoanalysis; possibly just as much to the interpretation of poetry; and the materials are threefold: fictive imaginings, dreams, memories, each subjected to association.

There follow two guides to going on (I hesitate to call them rules). 1. I must not close off the scope of the inquiry only because it seems to get very complicated by the introduction of ever-new materials; for these, if I am right or anywhere near it, will justify themselves by proving they belong. 2. I ought not very much to resist the impulse to digress, or what looks like digress; that is, to introduce a new subject, even if it seems to come up by accident.

For, apart from whatever else is happening, there is going forward an investigation into the nature of forms; assbackward from the procedures of fiction, one doesn't plant clues to be cleared up by new information; instead, one introduces the new information because it is going to belong, it will clarify the preceding matters and so earn a place in the story.

All that shows how much, how very much, resistance I have to leaving for the moment the investigation of last night's dreams and yesterday's memories, neither of which show any sign of yielding to thought just now, in favor of introducing something else.

In the matter of the Profumo scandal, and the trial of Dr. Stephen Ward on charges of pimping, living off the earnings of prostitutes, there is a relation of sex, power, and art (Dr. Ward also an artist) which is related to the themes of these notes. And to something else: for in the same paper as reports the first there is an account of the condemning of *Fanny Hill* as an obscene publication (the two are actually related in the paper itself). I was sent a copy of the new edition of Cleland's work, now entitled *Memoirs of a Woman of Pleasure*, by the publisher, who invited my comment.

I now realize exactly why these two subjects occurred to me as relevant to my inquiry. But even I am a touch shocked, because the point involves the introduction of other people, the consulting of old newspapers; in short, research . . . which I dislike. So I shall refrain from pursuing the subject at this moment, and wait to find out if it is necessary.

A Dr. Kildare movie on TV I stumbled in on the end of, which put the problem of the historical against what is personal very awfully—a general, in hospital, asking what he had lived for, winning one war to produce a more frightful other one, finally pretending to be a doctor in order to hold the hand of his nurse's dying husband. . . . I cried over my father for an hour. My tears were saying that I did something terribly wrong in outliving him.

I haven't much heart for this tonight. I hate intelligence, and have nothing else.

But the point at which I broke off was the memory that my father had been caught in an incident having to do with call girls, perhaps ten years ago.

26 VII

An office full of counters separated by glass partitions. I am told that here one can buy newspapers from consulates all over the world.

The point of contact with the real world here is my unsuccessful attempt to look up that about my father, yesterday afternoon; if in the *Times Index* at all, it is heavily camouflaged; though I recall warning myself that given any chance at all I would overlook it. I realize now that there were several years during which I read the *Tribune*, and that the dream seems to mention this obliquely by giving me another word from the Roman official class, *consulate*; as though a disguise that wishes to be seen through.

Association to the dream; finding contraceptives in my father's bedside table. This flickeringly alludes to "separated by glass partitions."

Another thing, set up by "office," about yesterday's second dream (Number Two, you recall). "The office" is RAF slang for the pilot's cockpit(!?). In that dream, though I was not a pilot but a passenger I was able to see ahead. The other situation in which one looks straight ahead, with a strained attention to the opposite wall, is at stool. The counters separated by glass partitions are public toilets; that the partitions should be glass indicates my fascination with the process of excretion in others, while the association with contraceptives links together defecation and birth. Newspapers, one has sufficiently often observed, print shit, hence are toilet paper, and the art of letters is being dyslogistically viewed as the dirtying of paper. If I suddenly got very dignified and said "the art of letters" instead of just "writing," is that not conditioned by the fact that contraceptives were also called "French letters" (consulates all over the world)?

Being a passenger yet able to see ahead, as one is not on a commercial airliner, seems to reflect a wish to have the best of everything without responsibility. The situation may express my secret view of these writings. First, they are hopefully a way of looking ahead with respect to my vocation as a writer. Second, I, as a self, have abdicated and given the control to a pilot, that is, to the unconscious, to memories, dreams, fictional imaginings, and their associations. This pilot says that we are late, meaning that I should have done this before (I did make several abortive—yes, abortive, I said—attempts at some such thing before, over the years, but they were not serious or long-enduring like this one). The episode of the fart, in this context, means much what I said yesterday it did: Though my 'spiritual' musings turn into gross filth the dream tries to reassure me as to my reputation (not stink much).

A third situation in which one looks straight ahead is this one of sitting at the typewriter, being unable to write (frequently termed constipation by many people, and writer's cramp by me).

After last night's crisis of feeling, possibly because of it, I feel this morning some need to resume the ground covered, to sweep up all this together for a few minutes, and say, for what reassurance it can give, what I have been doing for the past two to three weeks and about a hundred of these pages (I warn myself against taking a census, though).

I began under a pseudonym, Felix Ledger, whom I had invented as a novelist in a novel and written two chapters or more about, twelve or thirteen years ago. But after a single page in which this person tried to talk in a literary way about novels, he got stuck, and when he picked up the subject again after a lapse of a couple of weeks in despair of ever doing anything again, he began talking about his relation with the art of writing. But really, even thus early, he was talking about *my* relation with the art of writing, and the pseudonym was already serving no real purpose. But I retained it for the writing of ten days' entries lettered A-J, and it automatically dropped out only with the first narration and inspection of a dream, and the consequent deepening of analysis, the greater intimacy demanded with the details of my own past, which then and since became the true subject. Nevertheless, those first pages were necessary, though perhaps the pseudonym was not; and it is notable that this fictive self confesses rather less fully than I do myself.

Felix Ledger (the name seems to mean "happy but strictly accountable" + "lecher") wrote about the basis of writing in fear. He spoke eloquently of the necessity for self-examination, a part of which he conducted in largely moralizing terms, making one or two moderately interesting discoveries and introducing the real subject, me. But he was constantly divagating into technical considerations, talking about money, justifying himself (myself), being 'literary,' and generally altogether a bit too clever. Then he began having 'ideas' for novels, or stories. But only for a few days was he able to convince me that he was really Henry James who would really write the stories; I was soon enough able to see that these stories were being invented solely for purposes of obfuscation, and to say, in effect, that a person so very clever as Felix Ledger would never have to write a story at all in order to be loved, admired, and highly paid. Moreover, by inventing stories which I was not going to write, he was causing me some embarrassment.

But I did not drop him on purpose. I had had on the desk for several days a note reminding me that I wanted to write something "on the subject of memory"—my memory is so poor as to need a memorandum even of that. And when I had the dream about *Don Giovanni*, I suddenly began writing as myself, without Felix. At the time, perhaps I regarded the dream and analysis as merely an interruption; but it now appears as though Felix Ledger has gone. The subsequent entries are arranged and grouped by date rather than in an alphabetical sequence.

The first two dreams were able to be approached in a spirit of artistic play, coldly and with great energy. I should remember, through all this, that the investigation had the object from the beginning of getting me to write again, and that it was, and is now, a great pleasure to find so much strength liberated from melancholy and paralyzing despair, and to be once again interested in something. At the same time, I had uneasily the awareeness that life was going to get less agreeable; this awareness is reflected several times in the notes.

The first explosion of feeling was preluded by the examination of three dreams from the same night which did not yield much to investigation, and by the analysis of certain related memories, chiefly having to do with my sister and our early life at home; there was also the appearance of some new memories, the one about my father's disgrace and the one about the Rodin statue on the ashtray.

Then, suddenly, and provoked immediately, as if with design to humiliate my artistic pretensions, by a TV drama—Dr. Kildare . . . and tears, an hour of hysterical and punitive tears reproaching me for living after my father had died. This drama, though I didn't see by any means all of it, remains to be looked at more closely.

It hit me, I think, not only by the relation of the scene (a hospital, a dying man, &c.) to my father's last days, but by expressing so very nearly the doubleness in his nature and situation, a doubleness reflected in my own nature as well though perhaps not presently in my situation. A man of immense power and many powers, like the general in the play, who may—and this was a first revelation to me—who may have had and kept to himself a deep cynicism about life, about his life in particular, and who may have asked himself many times, perhaps with relation to his children, if the results of life had been worth living for.

                The general is gently reproached by an aged nurse whose husband is dying (these marvelous dramatic economies are so silly!); she tells him that his critique of history as responsible for the futility he feels about his life is but a disguise for his real occasion of despair, the feeling, or maybe the knowledge, that no one person has ever loved him, that he loves no one. Dr. Kildare (me?) looks on in stubborn agreement with this set of platitudinous but oh so terribly true statements. The general then finds his street clothes, poses as a doctor in order to get in to be with the nurse's husband in his last moments alive, holding the dying man's hand, imploring him to speak, saying in particular one thing, something like, "Only for a few minutes—we could be friends." That, I guess, is where I broke.

It is painfully necessary to add, though, that self-satisfaction creeps in: I have great difficulty in crying, though my crying when it happens tends to be loud, prolonged, and inconsolable, and regard the production of tears a little smugly, as the proffer of a guarantee to the human race that I belong.

There remains the impression of a vast historical guilt (for the general's criticism of life appears to me as having a certain truth) together with a personal anguish (for the one truth doesn't contradict the other) at never having known my father, at never having tried. One more predisposing factor: When I spoke of not having been able to find any record of the scandal about him, M reminded me that at the time I had a notion to call him and express my sympathy and affection in his trouble, but did not do so. Did not do so. Of course, it may partly have been that I was scared; what if it had been a quite different man with the same name? (Doubtful.) The subject was never mentioned subsequently. Even my good friends, I recall, took this doubtful way of showing their loyalty and supplying me with comfort: "Of course, we assumed it was another man entirely, with the same name." So that I had an excuse. But woe that I used it.

A dream partly evoked by this business, though, reflected back upon one of the recalcitrant dreams of the day before, and went some little way toward clearing up its meaning.

27 VII

Last night, something like five to eight dreams or scattered fragments of dreams (there were more, but these were all I noted in the dark); it is as if the wise old idiot within had said, "So he wants dreams, I'll give him dreams." I have a strong notion, even before beginning this morning's reflexions, that these riches are meant to constitute an embarrassment.

Association to that remark: Many years ago, I said in a lecture (and probably said many times after that) that historians formerly were hindered by the scarcity of documents; whereas now they are embarrassed by the immensity of the written record.

I have had for several days past the insistent thought that some sort of meditation about the pond has something to do with this exploration; the pond about which I wrote the poem, and which continues now to draw me to it with a daily fascination whose sense I haven't as yet attempted to make out.

There is also a hidden relation to the pond in reading this morning of the earthquake at Skoplje, about which I thought something like this: Well, that's the way it goes, this life. Here is one seismograph recording the tiny tremors of a distant vanity, the quakings of a dead child long years ago—and here, over the other side, balanced with this fat ego

minutely pirouetting, is a slight disturbance in which several
thousand persons were killed and many other thousands left
without shelter or food; all these were real live people, that
is, had to be counted by one and one and one, had lives deep
and intricate as the one herein being registered. . . . Think
of the smashing of that tremendous and delicate breathing
web of love affairs and robberies, litigations, promotions, fam-
ily feuds, divorces, surgery, convalescence, burial, birth, that is
a city (there, incidentally, is the center of the relation of this
thought with that of the pond, which I also think of as a
sort of city). In Skoplje perhaps a child was born who did not
live more than a few minutes until the city came down.

But
connected with such thoughts as this is also a kind of relief:
If there were suddenly an earthquake it would end at once
this painful searching among the ruins of the self. The two
thoughts side by side constitute the dialectic which says that
life is infinitely valuable and (because) absolutely valueless.

Associated with that is this thought about civilization. At
one moment, angels bear thee up, lest at any time thou dash
thy feet against a stone; there are lap robes, hot water bottles,
tea and biscuits, the best is none too good. The next moment
it's a loud, jeering voice: "Don't you know there's a war on?"

If what I am doing here has any prospect of revealing a form,
a species of narration less dull than I presently find fiction,
yet more hugely architectural than lyric poetry, this form has
also to be defined with reference to the things it isn't. The
temptation, I observe, is to be drawn away into pure auto-
biography, on the one hand, the external and more or less
chronological narrative of what happened; or, on the other
hand, into random reflexions, not much inspected with ref-
erence to the center, something like a notebook. Neither is

anything but a parody of what I intend, or a failure to accomplish what I intend. The principle that everything is relevant, simply because it comes into my mind, remains the principle of this work, but a principle which must get its justification daily so far as this is possible. It would appear, for example, that my dream-life is pretending to cooperate in the adventure by supplying an abundance of materials, but really trying to put a stop to it by giving me more than I can handle in a working day.

On thinking of this, I thought perhaps I would so devote myself to this work that I had no life outside it at all. And that I would call it *The Interior Hovel.* But when I tried to identify the real equivalent to St. Teresa's *Interior Castle* I saw at once it was the bathroom in our apartment, the bathroom in the interior, having no windows. That perhaps is why the hall where the elevator was came to me as so sinister; and I recall saying to A at grandpa's funeral that the most horrible thing about the chapel was its having no windows.

1. A girl named Dorothy A—— is coming to lunch, she has something to do with publishing. I go out in the car to look for her, it is raining, I nearly have an accident, slamming into another car's side so that the knuckles of my *right* hand are hurt. Then, beginning to climb a hill, with impatient drivers behind me, I find to my horror that the car won't move, something's wrong with the transmission. I put it into low gear, which I have never used, and am relieved to see that it goes, but I have to push very hard on the pedals.

Note. This is my present car. It is true I have never had to use the low gear, which is primarily for emergencies, getting stuck in sand, mud, on snow, &c. Two items make it plain that a kiddy-car is intended: the pushing on the pedals to make it go; the fact that it is so small I can drive with my right hand over the far edge. I suspect there may have been in my childhood a potty-chair shaped like a car, but do not remember this. (Having an accident, that is, fouling oneself, and being slapped on the hand? Transmission = bowel movement?)

2. Playing tennis indoors (gym, armory) with ———. I make a shot, he flies or climbs high and far into the rafters beneath the roof, and almost makes the return.

3. The Three Stooges. A line perhaps of soldiers. Larry, standing in this line, is slapped by Moe.

4. An emblem made of iron objects lying on the ground. Its meaning is: Grandma in the kitchen.

5. Going to the beach. I am staying with a German family(?), my car is parked in a restricted street but blocked fore and aft by two other cars, one of them shaped like a camel(?) or whale(?). When they move, I am able to drive my car away toward the beach, and when I return there is an open parking space, perfectly legal though on the left side of the street.

6. In a room with a boy who hands me a "30-20" rifle. I shake it to prove it has no bullets, and send him out to buy some.

7. The truck has arrived with lunch for B and his publishers. We are in a sort of clubhouse. M and I somehow force them to invite us for lunch.

I observe about analysis that there are two kinds, false and true. The false would be satisfied with the academic statement of the past in relation to theory: I might perceive, say, that I wanted to kill my father and sleep with my mother, and, perceiving this, be no more shocked than by wanting to go to the movies (I committed myself to a comparison—no more shocked than—and waited a long, anxious moment before deciding on one that would be innocuous and give nothing away).* This false analysis, that is, generalizes the position, it speaks reassuringly of Everyman not of oneself. The true, on the other hand, does not rest till it elicits the horrifyingly personal imagery in which one's predicament first and subsequently appeared. This is, too, you might say, the relation between academic poetry and real poetry.

Obvious that seven dreams or fragments of dreams is too many. It is a related characteristic in my attitude toward fiction that I often have too many ideas, so that I am paralyzed in trying to decide among them, so that one intrudes on and breaks up the unity of another, &c. It is as though the ucs. were saying: See, you haven't lost your creative powers, you can produce seven dreams in a night, a dozen ideas for stories in a single day, why, you are a giant among men! (All that is a metaphorical reassurance about sexual powers, too.) In this way I prevent myself from giving a full allegiance to any one thing. I have often had a similar thought about my many temptations to infidelity: On the one hand, it must be that I do not really love my wife, or I would not have these many temptations. On the other hand, the multiplicity of the temptations acts generally as a guarantee against my doing anything real about any one of them. (In this context it is illuminating, though a rather dark illumination at that, to recall

* A rejected term: than by wanting to read a newspaper. But both do give something away, don't they? Seeing a movie relates to the discussion of seeing (photography) of a few days ago, with its specific assault on photography; the meaning of newspapers in my phantasy was also described a day or so back.

the equation, sometime ago, that said the novel = marriage while poetry = infidelity.)

Note now the much-increased tendency for this writing to return on itself, reflect back on its own past, delight in self-quotation. By this means it perhaps expresses itself as formally analogous to its subject, the going back into the past, the bringing up again of what has already been. Perhaps one might predict that this tendency, apparently in opposition to the tendency always to introduce new materials, is really complementary to it, and will gradually take over the composition with the effect ultimately of concluding it (everything will one day have been said twice), so that what began at random achieved a form at last, in retrospect having a clearly perceptible beginning, middle, and end; though I suspect we are far from that point just now.

Only one dream, and that the first, is told in much detail; and it is the one that evoked associations. The others seem largely inert. I do not know anyone named Dorothy A——. The initials are my sister's, Dorothy is the name of a cousin with whom I was once very friendly but whom I did not see for maybe twenty years until my father's funeral. Alan is the name of my sister's husband. The last dream of the series has more in common with the first than any of the others have with either or each other: publishing, lunch, car-truck (driving); and B was once very close to my cousin Dorothy.

The doubt about camel or whale in 5 comes from *Hamlet* III.2. One term is missing: The cloud under discussion may also be a weasel. The dream could be saying rather cryptically, about this account, "Then will I come to my mother by and by." Which expression, I can now see, would be as much as to say, "All this about dreams, about whether a car is a whale or a camel, is a lot of irrelevant blather, behind which you perceive, like Hamlet, the real burden of the old man's message: You have to get to the subject of Mother.

But that is extremely ingenious isn't it? Symbolism itself is a suspiciously randomized way of sweeping the world up together and making it compassable as a single thought; it reaches, it swings far out on a slender thread to make its web.

Something about the metaphors I used there draws my attention. Compassable reminds me that this morning I thought of the compass rose, and that enough resembles the spider's web. The comparison of the compass rose and the rose of the blessed in Dante many years ago struck me as poetically striking. At the center of the spider's web sits the spider; at the center of the divine flower sits the mother of God; these thoughts come up immediately after the introduction of my mother by way of the dream-thoughts, and my dismissal of these as too clever and opportunist; now I note that my mother is also named Gertrude. (What, then, to complete the series, is at the center of the compass rose? Nothing. A blank. Association: the eye of the hurricane.)

Association, somewhat arbitrary, to 3. The three stooges are the three children, myself and my two sisters. A doubt whether there were not at one time four stooges. Memory that there was at one time, briefly, a fourth child, another son, died at birth or soon thereafter. *Hamlet* related to a German play *Der Bestrafte Brudermord*. A child dying at birth has already entered this morning's thoughts with reference to the earthquake at Skoplje, twice: "quakings of a dead child long years ago," which I thought was an awkward expression of 'the child I was, who is dead in me'; and "a child was born who did not live more than a few minutes until the city came down."

Now I can see a little why I am impelled to write about the pond. About a dozen years ago I wrote a poem called "The Pond." * It was a narrative about the pond near my house, what the books later taught me to call "a sterile, eutrophic pond." (At this instant the stranger on business from Porlock is here; I've told him to wait five minutes.) The poem was highly descriptive, or naturalistic, but its essence, the story, was a fiction, a phantasy, about a child named Christopher who drowned in the pond, which consequently was named after him. My constant phantasy these days about the pond, seeing the reflexion of the sun in its oil-black surface morning after morning, is that 'the sun is in the pond,' which I now see as a way of saying 'the son is drowned in the pond.' The other day I was trying to write a poem about watching the eclipse of the sun reflected in the pond, and in the poem I connected with the eclipse two signs and portents; seeing on the road "a squashed frog or small crucified man," and the coincidence that G just then returned from an antique-collecting trip with a huge crucified Christ; it was lying on the lawn, his children were fastening it to its cross, where the God's genitals should have been someone had driven in a rusty nail.

I'll leave this now. The man from Porlock is actually my good friend F, who helped me on the occasion which came first in this series of memories, when I broke my foot on the tennis court. The name of the poem was to have been "Coincidences," beginning with that of the sun and the moon which eclipsed it, or Father eclipsed by Mother in the preoccupations of these notes.

* Reprinted at the end of this text.

An hour later, I return to see if I can't see this more slowly, spread it out a bit more fully.

I said before that symbolism was 'suspiciously randomized'; this did not quite catch the thought. Isn't it rather that symbolism is insufficiently randomized to give account of the real world in its immense complexity? That symbolism acts as a reassurance that the world is small, accountable, inter-referential, echoing, inwardly allusive, the world of childhood where what happened was marvelous or terrible but bounded by the home, the park, the family? The world of religion, too, where what happened was marvelous or terrible but bounded by the situation of the divine drama. I see those insane Crusaders sailing slowly to Outremer. . . .

And that too is a thought of the pond, which is like a strange inland sea. The children used to sail there on rafts made of sledges from the paper mill (which makes toilet paper) and old inner tubes; the fashion passed, but a few whitened inner tubes, a few rafts, remain along the borders.

A few days ago, this notion of a children's story about the pond. The meadow and marsh around it are inhabited by children six inches high who can understand the language of animals and birds and fish and even insects. They go into houses at night to steal matches for torchlight parades which protect them from their enemies the owls.

My fascination with the pond has always been a fascination with a miniature world, one small enough to be observed and reported by a single intelligence, a kind of natural art work. But also a teeming full creation, growing every year more wild, more fierce with life, more manifold in species, exfoliating a domestic jungle not without its sinister aspect, connected with the amount of killing that goes on there through the summer days. But I myself have killed there, in a dream, a poem where I drowned a child named the Christ Bearer, whose name was given the pond, and whose death is thus heroic (a hero = one who dies for his people) so that he becomes the eponymous ancestor of all that multitudinous life and death. This child is my dead or stillborn brother? Was it that morning I remembered as the morning of the birth of one of my sisters?

That poem was about naming. I chose the name of Christopher without much thought (one of G's boys is named Christopher, but I didn't know them so well at the time). The poem connects poetry itself with naming, naming with sacrifice. In identifying the art of poetry with naming I say my own name (the poet is the *namer of* the world). In some sense it appears that I symbolically killed my brother, giving him the name of Christopher as a distorted and ambiguous indication that he 'bore Christ,' where bearing has the sense of birth, or that he was Christ, whom I killed (this thought will bring me in time to Jewishness, which has hovered around the edge of this morning's narration for some hours now), or that I was Christ.

All this is not without its reference to *Hamlet,* on which see the theory propounded in the Library Scene of *Ulysses.* (These notes at their very beginning said that *Ulysses* was the *crucial* moment in the history of novel-writing.)

Jewishness. In putting down dream 3, I had the passing thought that Larry was 'the Jewish-looking one' (they may all be, they may none of them be, I don't know). And I wrote a poem alluding to Herbert's "The Sacrifice" in its form, but making its hero Ahasuerus the Wandering Jew, who slapped

Christ. No he didn't, that's a false trail, he spat on Christ; I must be trying too hard.

An intermittence: when F came round, this morning, and I wrote about *coincidence*, there turned up a remarkable one in our subsequent conversation: I told him, hoping he might help B get a place during the coming year, of what has happened to B's husband: operated on, malignant brain tumor, fell ill while stationed at the Embassy in ———. F somewhat flabbergasted, said that a friend of his, a different man, had recently died of a malignant brain tumor; he was stationed at the same embassy.

Under the stress of this kind of writing the whole world becomes magical in quality; it has been clear for some days now that there exists in me a desire to treat 'real life' by the same associative and interpretative process I am applying to dreams. It has occurred to me that one test of method relevant to what is going on will be to 'interpret' with reference to my own past various mental products, for example, a made-up dream, someone else's dream, a novel or short story, a happening in real but waking life (such as my cold, already so interpreted).

I am reminded, as a friendly warning it may be, of a beloved passage from *Death in Venice*, describing how classicism, conscious and deliberate mastery, "moral fibre," may result in "a dangerous simplification, in a tendency to equate the world and the human soul, and thus to strengthen the hold of the evil, the forbidden, and the ethically impossible." Consider what happened to Aschenbach, also as a consequence of looking upon a divine child.

Associations with the pond. Seeking a metaphoric expression of it, rejecting 'machine,' I said it was a fire. Later on, an oil

fire (on account of the oily blackness of its surface). Allusions
to fire: the children with matches, the sun drowned in the
pond and burning there, burning gold. The fire of life, what
the poem called life "turning its inward heat upon itself."
Also as a city (Skoplje?): The creatures "peopled thick the city
of themselves." I remember, too, a theory that life began,
not in the sea as often supposed, but in fresh-water ponds.
Taking these references together with what has already been
said on this subject, it begins to appear that the pond is the
mother (the earth mother, erda, herta, the hearth, name re-
lated to Gertrude).

One "final, featuring blow" (what Melville calls the oper-
ation of Chance on the fabric of fate and freedom) for this
morning. There is now an otter in the pond. I seem to re-
member a story of Saki's in which a child dies and turns into
an otter.

       I was right and wrong. It is a girl named Laura, not
a child, who turns into an otter and is killed in that form.
But she had already said that after being killed as an otter
she would turn into a child, and she does, reappearing as "a
little beast of a naked brown Nubian boy."

Pure coincidence, of course. To think otherwise brings insan-
ity very near, though it would be a most artistic kind of in-
sanity. But let us be perfectly outrageous and list a couple of
other coincidences around the edges. Saki was the pseudonym
of H. H. Munro. I began these notes under a pseudonym.
Munro is structurally an inversion or simple anagram of my
own name. It bears the same relation, or nearly, to my name,
as the primitive form of Telemachus, Telmah, does to Hamlet
(another Son seeking the Father). This last piece of informa-
tion comes from Nabokov (another attempt to say my name?)
and it was in reviewing a story of his that I quoted his de-

scription of what I characterized as "poet's disease," that is, the compulsion to believe that every detail in the landscape is talking about you, and saying, moreover, bad things. Finally, the book in which Nabokov wrote that clever thing about Telmah-Hamlet was *Bend Sinister*. Was I really conceived illegitimately?

Doubtless the philosophers can explain (away) such strange constatations of fact, these little, mad galaxies far out in space where some intellectual divinity is fooling with the idea of genesis.

As Munro alludes to my name sort of backward, so my phantasy that the drowned child of the poem became an otter (who will eat up the other wildlife of which the child is the ancestor) is the reverse of what happens in Saki's story "Laura."

Enough. Or too much.

1. I am at a hotel in Alaska. In the morning I have to catch a plane, and there are delays in elevators, with girls taking me to the wrong floor. Then I have difficulty making out the check, my hand trembles, the writing looks like someone else's. The check is made out to the proprietress of the hotel. On the way to the airport I realize that I have left my coat behind, and wake in anguished indecision whether to continue or go back. The plane was to leave at 9:30. The check was for $187.50.

2. The apricot opened, (he) (she) fell out of the helicopter and was killed.

The second clause came to me as a line of verse. It is connected with someone's taking a news photograph of something—a waste basket?—atop the pylon of a bridge; also with the thought that the photographer didn't really climb up there, he used a helicopter, so it was neither difficult nor dangerous; then with the thought that although helicopters were pretty safe, you could if you were foolish enough or enough preoccupied (with the camera, for instance) fall out of one.

Associations to all this: Margaret Bourke-White. News photo a couple of days ago of a helicopter—true, an experimental one—that did crash, killing pilot and passenger as well as someone in a car.

If you took, as I did at first, the second dream without the associations, there is a simple and doctrinaire way of reading it straight through as a wish not to have this child, of either sex. The apricot is the female genital, the helicopter the womb. But the dream is ingenious in linguistically complicating the meaning by puns. "Apricot" was once "apricock," as in "Go bind thou up yon dangling apricocks" (*Richard II*, III.4, cf. "came to me as a line of verse"), bringing in the male genital as well. Helicopter contains "helix" or spiral, that is, "screw," but is sometimes misspelled and mispronounced "heliocopter," giving the thought of the sun (son).

The associations combine a photographer (sister) with Margaret (wife). The dream-thoughts form an ingeniously nasty compound, wishing that my wife would die in childbirth in order that I might marry my sister; saying that this indeed might happen (helicopters, and hospitals, are pretty safe, and yet here is this news photo of a helicopter that did crash, leaving the inference clear). Killing pilot and passenger translates as mother and child, but also as myself (represented as pilot and passenger, unconscious and ego, in a dream several days ago), and this thought may be stressed by the vague addition of "as well as someone in a car," corresponding by repetition to "the *apri*cot *opened*" of the beginning. The entire passage from *Richard II* is frighteningly relevant:

> Go bind thou up yon dangling apricocks,
> Which, like unruly children, make their sire
> Stoop with oppression of their prodigal weight. . . .

The secret reading of this would be that the apricocks and sire represent scrotum and penis. Whether as wish or fear, "bind thou up" has the surgical sense of "tie off." The thought is simple enough, behind its complicated poetry: I seem to attribute my sexual apathy to children; the sire, the penis, cannot erect himself to royalty and pleasure because of the weight of the balls, signifying the subservience of his pleasure to generation. Also, an army doctor (the Gardener, in *Richard II?*) told me long ago that I might have trouble with the scrotum (varicocele), but I never have had.

What frightens most of all is that the thoughts *are* interpretable. A word in the dream suggests a line in Shakespeare, three lines in Shakespeare. I interpret (as I suggested yesterday that I might do) these three lines in application to myself, this interpretation is utterly false if you consider what the lines mean in the play, yet consistent at the same time, and as true to my situation as false to the play's—which is, however, about a deposed king, the imagery of his plight in the scene under consideration being drawn from unruly vegetation, a garden grown wild, and full of words with a heavy sexual charge. I cannot but see that this scene refers me to the pond, and add a further link, that helicopter = dragonfly, the latter also a character in the poem and in at least two related poems.

Interpretation as simultaneously false and true. A long way back in these notes I was compelled to say that whenever I made a distinction it was sure to collapse, that is, seem true and then reveal itself as false. And yesterday my memory of Saki's story was "both right and wrong." Now I must add a further instance in this category. I did look up the Kierkegaard aphorism vaguely recalled in relation to my dream about *Don Giovanni*, and the same balance of true and false obtains. It is in the Diapsalmata, not the Preface:

> I divide my time as follows: half the time I sleep, the other half I dream. I never dream when I sleep, for that

would be a pity, for sleeping is the highest accomplishment of genius.

So I was substantially right about what he wrote, but wrong about the sense in which he wrote it, if I meant to justify my dreaming instead of writing fiction.

Looking at Kierkegaard, whom I haven't read for so many years, may have produced the fear that he had already written this book of mine, which issues in Dream 1 as "the writing looks like someone else's." I quote now for a kind of motto the first sentence of his Preface, which seems to me exquisitely appropriate just now:

> Dear Reader: I wonder if you may not sometimes have felt inclined to doubt a little the correctness of the familiar philosophic maxim that the external is the internal, and the internal the external.

Yes, I do doubt a little. And among yesterday's notes is one to speak of false and true analysis, the one doctrinaire, or rationalist, the other personal and as it were historical, corresponding to the guidance of Virgil and the guidance of Beatrice.

The spider sets up the geometric coordinates of his web with smooth thread. Then he fills in the pattern with sticky thread to hold his victims, and to do this he must first take out some of the smooth threads.

With that I hit an unidentified obstacle. One part of me wants to go on wrestling with the dream. Another part says that is just the way to get nowhere; you should look for a way around, another point of attack. Still another: Something descriptive, about the pond in particular, would be artistically a relief from all this 'analysis.'

I walked down past the pond, thinking of these things. All at once there came to mind five associations to that pond, and at that moment the strap of my sandal broke, though not until some minutes later did I remember the strap of the sandal in my childhood portrait. Here are the associations, three from childhood, two from literature and later on.

1. Lily Pons, coloratura. 2. Rosa Ponselle, contralto. 3. Pond's Cold Cream, which Mother used to rub into her face at night, giving her skin, when I went to kiss her goodbye in the morning, a white, greasy shine and a particular smell I am unable to describe. 4. A few years ago, writing on the nature of poetry, I made up a fable in which the drowned Narcissus speaks about poetry as the contemplation of, the dying into, the imagery of the pond. 5. Many years before that, in my first, unpublished novel, *From the Old World*, is a vision of a pond as the source of variously malformed human lives.

I observe once more the characteristic form which my disability takes. I am being overwhelmed, as though on purpose, with more materials than I can deal with, and I respond as usual by jumping ineffectually from one to another, just so as not to lose any of them. But in this way I insure also that I can't really have any of them.

Another thing. Yesterday I yielded to my dream-expressed fear of losing both copies by fire, and sent one copy to the secretary to be typed over. This decision means ascribing value to the ms. as a possession, a piece of property, and inspires natural doubts that instead of liberating myself from the past I am merely burdening myself with a new version of it.

On the other hand, it is a hopeful sign that I did not simply stop this morning, but actually made significant progress in dealing with the second dream and the associated lines from Shakespeare.

One of the things stopping me just now is the feeling that I must order, group, and above all criticize, the impressions of this work. Putting this off, unwilling to copy into the record such things as the speech of Narcissus or the vision of the pool, I was wandering through old journals and notebooks, where I was suddenly hit by the relevance of this criticism (5 VII 53):

> B called on me this morning, not because of my having called yesterday while he was out—this he did not know—but because he had vaguely asked E by letter when we might be arriving, and E, with whom we have had no communication of any sort since last August, replied with the certainty of absolute ignorance that we would get here on the weekend of the fourth. This is the way in which things happen, the direct and rational communication fails, no one looks at it once much less twice, and it is replaced by an extremely improbable, random, and very complex concatenation of accidents.

That represents accurately enough the sort of mistrust I have been experiencing all day of the analyses, or, say, rather, constructions, of yesterday and this morning. I think I shall knock off this work for a time.

29 VII

An often repeated thought while looking at the pond: You might blind yourself even by staring at the image of the sun drowned there.

It ties in the phantastic theorizing about photography (seeing) with the guilty thought given fictive and permissible expression in the poem, about a child (my brother?) drowning in the pond; and the greasy shine of Pond's Cold Cream on mother's face in the morning replicates the greasy shining scum on the surface of the pond as I see it every morning, with the sun rising opposite and inescapably reflected to me. It is part of the thought that the real danger of blinding oneself is becoming hypnotized by the image of the sun. I suppose the doctrinaire identification of blindness with castration is worth a pious mention here.

Even the mirror might not save Our Hero from being turned to stone. My poems, S wittily said, are "about history from the point of view of the losers," and in one of them I write about myself not as Perseus, but as an anonymous "Predecessor of Perseus."

A day of doubts, hesitations, and perplexities concerning this work. I shall try to detail the form these take.

The game of the novel, that cruel initiation rite described earlier, isn't that exactly what I have been playing with myself? By means of slender filaments of association, remote and sometimes purely grammatical linkages, paranoiac assertions of a hidden guilt in the most obvious and trivial images of daily life, I have been building up certain structures; to what do these structures correspond? Do they, for example, have the nature of self-discovery? Or are they not, instead, discoveries of a fictive self corresponding—as in that game—to my fears about my own character rather than that character itself? Answers to questions which no one has asked, no one, that is, except myself, except myself. . . .

Agreed, it is the way of the mind to proceed by associations, and with a little natural aptitude for listening you can hear the subtlest echoes of likeness. And it is the habit of the mind to ascribe these resemblances to the nature of things perceived by the mind, and not to the laws of the mind's working alone, not to language alone. There is the hope, as Richard Wilbur wrote, that in the happiest intellection a graceful error may correct the cave.

It may be altogether appropriate, though, that is, artful, that an attempt to find out why I cannot write fiction should turn into an attempt to tell the truth about myself, which in its turn is turning into a fiction about myself, the very self who a moment ago could not write fiction. The atoms of memory have hooks at either end; the bits and pieces of a life, taken one by one and in no apparent order, or in an order arbitrarily determined, are nevertheless demonstrated to express themselves in accordance with a law, or a design, and to form some sort of coherent picture when viewed from the right distance. This picture may be utterly fictive, or metaphorical. And I may be able to put down its elements, and order these, without ever myself understanding the design that emerges (a trained psychoanalyst, for example, would probably read my dreams and other accounts in a quite different way), without ever myself achieving the right distance, at which the fragments would blend into a picture according to the law of their association.

You could not apprehend relation at all without a language, without terms. But these terms then seem to impose upon you the quality of the relations you apprehend by their means. For example, I could not have proceeded upon this investigation in the way that I have without the knowledge of some things discovered and/or invented by Freud. But the names of these discoveries impose themselves upon my approach to the objects, memories, feelings, images, I try to deal with, and condition the nature of my apprehension of them (my apprehensions about them, too, very likely). It is an obvious danger of this psychoanalytically conditioned adventure that the mind begins its interpretations with an a priori determination to find symbolisms and associations having to do with sex, childhood, the family romance, excrement. That doesn't mean that what turns up is necessarily false, but it does create a danger of being doctrinaire, of taking short cuts to 'meaning,' the short cuts especially of symbolism, which cause the mind to miss more personal and probably painful discoveries of deeper connexions which might have been seen on the longer way round. As a friend said, so many years ago, with a delightful air of seeing the meaning only just after hearing the saying, "A phallic symbol is anything longer than it is wide."

In confirmation of the above, the frequent assertion that Freudian patients dream Freudian dreams and Jungian patients dream Jungian dreams. In the former it is Friday night, probably during Passover, the whole *maspocha* is there, even one or two known to be dead; grandpa comes up smiling, the light glinting off his gold-rimmed glasses, opens your mouth and quickly, as you wake up, takes out a tooth. In the latter, you are in a white marble courtyard with a pool and fountain at the center, a cypress grove behind; a lady in a long white gown beckons from beyond, and a voice not hers says to you "*Lux aeterna luceat eis, domine,*" though you are not a Catholic and don't know Latin.

Now I 'made these up.' Or they 'came to me.' And they are not dreams, but daytime fictions. Still, according to the theory of this book they should be interpretable. And according to Freud they should turn out to be two versions of the same thought.

Our relation to experience is dominantly genitive: *my* sickness, *my* enemy, *my* death. We possess everything that posesses us. But even the occurrence of that thought may belong to the two pseudo-dreams: 'Dominantly' is the echo of 'domine' a moment before.

Of course it is nonsense to say that those two examples are either interpretable or alike. But it is the purpose of the inquiry to push to extremes, so I shall try anyhow, though I have a considerable unwillingness to do so. This unwillingness expressed itself as laziness, fatigue, feeling the heat, so that I went downstairs and took a shower and shave before sitting down to this again; let us begin by saying that the white marble court with fountain and pool is the bathroom with shower and toilet. Does it have to do also with the mouth and tooth of the first dream?

Both 'dreams,' different as they are in detail and especially in tone (which was by design, of course), have in common religious observance; in one it is Passover, in the other someone recites a phrase about the dead, from the Requiem Mass. My grandfather is dead (both of them are, but I think especially of my mother's father), so that the light on his gold-rimmed glasses may be the translation into fact of the wish that eternal light may shine on the dead.

More phantastically still, the white marble courtyard with pool and fountain is the expansion of the dentist's bowl and fountain where you rinse; grandpa acts as a dentist when he takes out your tooth. The lady in white, beckoning, is the nurse telling you that the dentist can take you now. The cypress grove belongs to Grandpa by his association with Florida and the Everglades, also to death by means of Böcklin's picture of the Isle of the Dead. Going to the dentist was always an occasion of fear, adapted in the dreams to the expression of the fear of death (losing a tooth = losing oneself; never mind about castration just now, please, no matter what we know about symbolism and Cleopatra's dream book) in relation to religious questions. Being with the whole family, living and dead, is identified with Jewishness, while the lonely and absurdly exalted pseudo-mysticism of the second, where death gets landscaped romantically, belongs to Catholicism. I am not a Catholic, but came close to being converted at least once while in college, on some such foolish ground as that it was a much more artistic and beautiful religion than Judaism (red hats and old masters, I guess); after my father's death I made my sister a present of a recording of the Mozart Requiem, with a strange idea (never expressed aloud) that she might find it appropriate. It is my favorite piece of music, I suppose, in part because of the strange story told of the circumstances of its composition. Also, I really don't know Latin, though I am able to read simple and brief expressions, tags, proverbs, church Latin, am acquainted with the Mass, &c., and have always been embarrassed about this. (I did well in Latin at school, but realize I was badly taught; which is worth mentioning because it is balanced in the Jewish dream by the fact that I was taught Hebrew for purely ritual purposes, my Bar-mitzvah, and don't understand that language either.)

So the two dreams, which I made up broad waking, do respond to interpretation, and do reveal a number of similarities, as well as indicating some oppositions which distinctly inform me they have to be read as a single dream having a single thought. This thought might be expressed in a number of strata, but so far as I can see it goes somewhat as follows: For a Jew, death is nothing to fear, the whole family is with you, even the process of dying (the extraction) is done by the dearest old ineffectual in the household, who smiles as he does it (and who has died himself, which shows you it's not so difficult). If you became a Catholic, on the other hand, you would go alone, as to the dentist, there would be something fake in the artistry, the pictorial style, of dying this way, and even when the priest expressed a wish that light eternal should shine on the dead, hence on you (or *eis*, them = the family?), you would only feel embarrassed and out of place because you didn't really belong (are not a Catholic) and don't even understand the language, the dead language or language of the dead, in which he says this.

At another stratum, the thought is: Better off with the Jew Freud, tell your dreams in his style; with him, taking out a tooth is really taking out a tooth, he tells you life is tough and doesn't promise anything; while Jung, the Christian mystagogue, will give you a lot of Hollywood death imagery that looks consoling but will turn out to be the same old savagery in the end.

The relation of this work to Freud is expressed in what I told my students, that I was teaching them "The Poetics of Everyday Life."

The two made-up dreams surprised me a good deal by responding to interpretation; surprised me so much, in fact, that I became suspicious of so easy a victory, and began to wonder if perhaps it was not designed to prevent my looking further into the matter.

For example, dentist and Catholic priest are metaphorically identified in my first published novel, *The Melodramatists* (1949), by a girl who is contemplating conversion. The priest says that for her to relapse after baptism "would be a tragedy I am anxious to avoid." And she thinks, "How like a dentist he is, after all . . . (that this wisdom tooth should become impacted is a tragedy I am anxious to avoid)."

Two realms of the made-up dreams, dentistry and religion, are united in the epithet: wisdom tooth.

With this, a cluster of memories arises, beginning with a dentist who was said, with what truth I am uncertain, to have treated our family free of charge after my father had talked him out of killing himself. If the story is true, he paid dearly for the privilege of living, for on my teeth alone he could have made thousands of dollars. In my reluctant dealings with this man (I was perhaps fifteen) it frequently crossed my mind that he wanted my teeth to outlast me, that I was his monument, those fillings would still be there when the last Pyramid had been worn down to the desert, and so on. Ideas of death and eternity in connexion with teeth appear thus early in my life, and it comes to me now that behind *"lux aeterna"* is the dentist's overhead light which I described in a short story (about a man who tried to kill himself) as "blinding from one angle, bland from any other," and compared to "a small dinosaur." ("Looking down your throat" is an expression of triumphant aggression and hostility, chiefly in poker games.)

Our family doctor also had a light, a little pencil-affair, and looked down one's throat when one was ill. This man, who brought me into the world and saw me through the numerous sicknesses then routine for children, gave me a physical exam just before I went to college, of which I remember two things. He took hold of my penis for an instant, in a purely professional way, and made some remark of amused approval. But this was accompanied by a kind of surrogate intimacy: He confessed to me that he was a Communist, or at least that he approved the doctrine, but asked me to keep this a secret as it wouldn't do his practice any good for it to be known. He had another secret, which he kept until a few weeks before his death: that he had cancer. His daughter, with whom I went out a couple of times, has the same name as the girl in my novel.

These associations are all such as diverge from the dreams; they don't converge on the meaning, and don't yet invite another reading. But there is something else I wanted to consider as part of the two made-up dreams; that is, that before trying to interpret them I said something apparently unrelated, about our relation to experience being "dominantly genitive." Then I remarked that this statement might have been part of the dreams because "dominantly" was influenced by "*domine*" in the second dream.

Dominantly genitive seems to express the compound of fighting and love-making alluded to in several images and memories: the Syrian statuettes, Rodin's "Le Baiser" thought of as the counterpart to the statue of the panther and python in combat, and so on. It occurred to me as I put down the thought that grammar was full of sexy words: genitive (which still has the second meaning of genital), conjugate, copula; even 'active' and 'passive' are capable of being thought of this way.

But all this too remains obstinately far from the two dreams.

MUD TURTLE

Out of the earth beneath the water,
Dragging over the stubble field
Up to the hilltop in the sun
On his way from water to water,
He rests an hour in the garden.

Everyone observes his alien presence,
His lordly darkness bannered in filth,
Streaming his weeds like a lady's favor;
He is a black planet, another world
Never till now appearing, even now
Not quite believably old and big,
Set in the brilliant morning's midst
A gloomy gemstone to the sun opposed.

Our measures of him do not matter,
He would be huge at any size;
And neither do the number of his years,
The time he comes from doesn't count.

When the boys tease him with their sticks
He snaps the sticks, striking with
As great a suddenness as speed.
And when they turn him on his back
To see his belly heroically yellow,
He hurls himself fiercely to his feet,
Brings down the whole weight of his shell,
Spreads out his claws and digs himself in
Immovably, invulnerably,
But for the front foot on the left,
Red-budded, with the toes torn off.
So over he goes again, showing
Where a swollen slug is fastened
Softly between plastron and shell.
Nobody wants to go close enough
To burn it loose; he can't be helped
Either, there is no help for him
As he makes it to his feet again
And drags away to the meadow border.
We see the tall grass open and wave
Over him, it closes, he is gone
Over the hill toward another water,
Moving with gravity his black
Cavernous mount, his muddy weeds
Cracked in the mounting sun, he takes
A secret wound out of the world.

That poem has to go in there for several reasons (or those
madnesses I am consenting to call reasons within this work).

First, the turtle comes from the pond. Someone said the other day that there ought to be turtles in there, but I had never seen one out of it till this morning, and it represented at once a new and sinister depth of possibility in the image entire. Second, he made his appearance this morning, and I wrote him down this morning: something which is true of many of my poems. As though now and again one were absolutely ready for what turned up. Third, it is a law of this writing that what happens during it thereby becomes eligible for inclusion. And last, it is also a law of this writing that whatever turns up and is included, is taken metaphorically to have the same status as a dream; that is, it opens itself to the chance of interpretation.

The principle of the work once again, and more explicitly than before, asserts itself as magical, concerned with signs and portents, pushing to the extreme limit the claim of every art work to be the world, to be life. This extreme limit might be thought of as prophecy; I am behaving, with respect to metaphor, like that scientist who said, "I am surprised that I cannot remember the future." (William Francis Gray Swann, "What Is Time?")

Now my business is certainly not to interpret the poem in any 'objective' or critical style, seeking in the ordinary manner to arrive at a consensual reading which every right-minded person has to admit as being in the poem. I imagine there is such a reading, and it would turn up when teacher persuaded or coerced the students into an agreement on "what the poem says," after which he would magnanimously allow for tonal and other differences of opinion based on more or less remote and private associations in each individual. These differences, however, besides being infinite in number, are not of interest to criticism because criticism is largely consensual, the socializing of judgment.

But what criticism doesn't care about is exactly what I do care about: the delineation of readings—of anything, lives, dreams, poems, newspaper items—that shall satisfy these requirements: They are private, not public, and can be arrived at only by the individual on the basis of his own life, hence they differ from (and are crazy with reference to) the readings of public, objectively minded criticism. But at the same time they meet the demand of that criticism by being beautifully consistent with the text, while they express in addition an illumination of the individual life which could not have been arrived at by the ordinary methods.

It happens not by chance, perhaps, that I copied out and have kept for many years an example, the only one I have ever found, where substantially this happens in the course of public criticism; it refers to a great passage in *Macbeth* (1.7.16–25):

> Besides, this Duncan
> Hath borne his faculties so meek, hath been
> So clear in his great office, that his virtues
> Will plead like angels trumpet-tongu'd against
> The deep damnation of his taking off;
> And pity, like a naked new-born babe
> Striding the blast, or heaven's cherubim, hors'd
> Upon the sightless couriers of the air,
> Shall blow the horrid deed in every eye,
> That tears shall drown the wind.

Concerning this, T. R. Henn comments as follows (*The Apple and the Spectroscope*):

The whole passage is a remarkable illustration of the way in which personal considerations may intrude themselves. To a certain Bomber Pilot the whole imagery suggested the air and aircraft. *So clear in his great office* suggested the pilot, encased in Perspex: *the office* being slang for the cockpit. *Angels* suggested, phonetically, *engines*, and *trumpets* the roar of them preparatory to taking-off. Further, the codeword for "thousands of feet," in height, was *angels*; ten *angels* = ten thousand feet. *Taking off* needs no explanation. *Striding the blast* referred to the aircraft over the target, with the bomb-doors open; the *sightless couriers* a squadron flying at a great height in cloud. For him, the whole passage was linked to the pity and terror of night operations.

This will be the right place to put in the question one or another student will always ask during such a discussion: Was that Shakespeare's real intention? Was he conscious of all that? Aren't you reading things into the poem?

But our present object, it may be, is to read things into the poem in such a way that they stay there as the articulations of a world quite other than that the poet intended, was conscious of, and so on.

Probably, all the same, my interpretation of my own poem must begin with the visible simplicities, like any other, and diverge from the common run of possible interpretations only with the rising up of private associations, phantasies, memories. The question at the back of my mind, however, is: Why was it my lot to view the turtle in just this way? For, to put it in the simplest way, here was a pretty ordinary turtle, larger than I thought such beasts generally were hereabouts but by no means gigantic even so. The prose of the event might have run so: This morning there was a turtle on G's lawn. One of the boys phoned me because they all thought I'd like to see anything that came out of that pond.

We stood around for maybe ten minutes making remarks about the turtle, the boys poking experimentally at the turtle: The things that happened in the poem were in fact the things that happened: turning the turtle turtle, our observation of his wound, of the slug, and so forth. The poem differs from the facts solely by attitude, tone, and association (figurative language). But there is a very great difference, though that says nothing as to the merit of the poem.

This turtle of mine comes from the deepest depths, the deep beneath the deep, not only from underwater but from the mud under that; something I had not considered. His pilgrimage takes him up to the top of a hill in full sunlight, in a 'garden'; but he is headed down again, this is but a station on his journey from one dark to the next. I seem to feel him chiefly as a series of contradictions. He comes from hell, he is hell (lordly darkness = the dark lord), but there is something phantastically knightly (suggested by his armor) about him; his filth is also a chivalry. He is utterly 'alien' to our ideas of size and age, he is not quite believable, he is a paradoxical compound of utter sloth with terrible speed, of courage with cowardice ("his belly heroically yellow"), he is a black planet (knight *errant* = wanderer = planet), hence could not appear in darkness as other planets do, but only in the sunlight. He is a treasure of darkness, buried in earth (gemstone), he is "to the sun opposed," yet at the same time he climbs out of darkness to the height and then goes down, just like the sun; the action of the poem centers on turning him upside down and what then appears: that he is horribly wounded, that he suffers a parasite who sucks his life. The human beings can't damage him much, but when he becomes pitiful they can't help him either, because they are afraid. Disappearing at the end, he is stoical, carrying his damage in silence and with some dignity; he is an outcast, a sort of scapegoat, as if we had lost interest in him on perceiving that he was quite beyond our means either to help or hurt; and he is strangely a savior, "he takes A secret wound out of the world" as though it were somehow our guilt for his amputated foot, or as though he momentarily revealed to us something horrifyingly bitten and lost beneath the foundation of the world, something we were unwilling to contemplate for more than an instant, and which he obligingly took back into the dark with him, leaving us perplexed, maybe a little shaken, between the view of a natural thing and the vision of an emblem of the kingdom of darkness with its implacable hurt; as though all the pain in the whole world were but the audible equal of an agony suffered by the Old Dragon in silence and night.

Someone remarked (and all the others winced) that you could wade in the pond and lose your toes before you knew what happened. Quite possibly so; but this is also a common nightmare theme, and one which I feel with a particular horror. I now see that I quote that remark (but left it out of the poem) because it somehow belongs to the series of paradoxes that characterize the turtle, belongs as it were to the dream-thoughts, which say: This is the monster of darkness that eats toes. But in fact he is the one whose toes have been eaten.

All right. In one reading, he is the avenging spirit of the pond (the mother) where I drowned a child; he comes from a level deeper than I had contemplated ("something I had not considered"), he is the vagina dentata, and will castrate (because symbolically the child drowned in the pond is the penis dying in the mother). In this sense he is truly "to the son opposed." But he has an equal and opposite sense, for his toes are cut off, not mine, he is a substitute victim, he is the lost son (sun) who demonstrates immortality by coming again from the mother depths as the real sun does each morning, and he comes both wounded and armored to show me that one cannot emerge unscathed from primary experience, but that one can at least emerge, and with a certain lonely, ugly, heroic dignity that bears its wounds and asks nothing of anyone.

In the other poem the child drowned in winter, by falling through a hole in the ice. That is, the mother's coldness to the child was felt as his protection, the very ground he stood on; *melting* would be fatal to him. But I see the turtle's armor as responding to the ice on the pond, as a transformation of it. One goes into the watery deep, the mother, piercing the ice of her sexual indifference, and dies there. But one comes back from that darkness dirty and wounded but armored with as hard a substance as the ice itself, and wearing the filth of birth and death "like a lady's favor."

Without any contradiction, another reading makes out the turtle to be the father, wounded by life but having the power to wound the son (bite off his toes) in the same way. And the son, myself, is then grotesquely seen as a parasite on the father's life, a slug; but "nobody wants to go close enough to burn it loose." No one, not the same son, certainly, will approach the father at his weak spot to burn loose the creature who eats his life.

This inspires very mixed thoughts. Someone suggested burning the slug loose with a cigarette; smoking probably had something to do with my father's cancer; I say to myself helplessly that I smoke too much and will no doubt finish (be punished) in the same way. Smoking imitates sucking, but one sucks on fire; the nipple is dangerous, prohibited (don't play with fire, the child is told), also smoking is erotically attractive as having to do with growing up, doing (in secret) what the grownups do openly, and probably has some symbolic reference to masturbation, another sort of playing with fire. I remember again that in the Rodin replica the couple were embraced on the edge of an ashtray.

Looking again at the two made-up dreams and their associated memories and readings: The dentist's bowl where you rinse is equal and opposite to the baptismal font.

These notes tend to divide into the analysis of metaphors, on the one hand, and associational complexes, where it is safe to be brilliant, and on the other hand memories, which are not brilliant at all, and have about them something inert, stupid, and prospectively disagreeable; they thus represent again the struggle between the plausible and theoretical intelligence I pretend to be (the creature that doesn't exist = the unicorn) and the filthy, bestial child deliberately hidden from the light (= the minotaur).

And there, without any premeditation that I am aware of, I introduced something which I yesterday omitted from the poem and interpretation. About the turtle's armor I had been going to use the word 'horn,' and didn't, probably (or superficially) because I wasn't certain the substance of the shell was really the same as the substance of horn (or tooth?).

         I

have not been noting down my dreams for a couple of nights past, just because they gave me more than I could deal with. But last night I was compelled to remember a dream which in its most compact expression said only two words: Matterhorn, Automat. And this morning I started to characterize myselves in two opposed ways—and symbolized these as a one-horned and a two-horned creature. The associations of 'horn' are worth inspecting, but I warn myself that the inspection will not be easy, if only because so many things come to mind at once that it will take some patience to unfold them.

In expanded form the dream said something like: It would be clever of a novelist to symbolize the penis as 'the Matterhorn,' because of the many and complex puns involved in the name of that mountain, for example the horn of the mother, the horn from which matter comes. Then the dream said, But that is exactly the sort of cheap, superficial cleverness you complain about in yourself; you run your mind as though it were an Automat. 'Automat' appeared as a reversed resonance of 'Matterhorn,' but also through the association with 'Horn & Hardart' the proprietors, whom children of my time routinely referred to as 'Whore & Hard-on' (reminding me of Matthew Arnold's celebrated poem about a father killing his son in combat, which we used to call, in revenge for having to read it, Sore Ass & Rectum). If 'Matterhorn' is one way interpretable as speaking of the matter (sperm) that comes from the horn, then 'Automat' may very well refer to masturbation (mental masturbation, too, was a common expression for the sort of activity of the mind my dream disparages as being like an Automat). 'Horny' was, and is, slang for being sexually aroused and frustrated (hard up). True dreams are said to come through the gate of horn, as false through the ivory gate; that was Virgil, and in Dante, his pupil, you have the description of the demon farting, so curiously expressed as "he made a horn of his ass." Horns are the emblem of the cuckold, though no one seems to know just why (conjectures given in Lucas' edition of Webster). In connection with 'Automat' I observe that my dreams, not in the series here reported only, are highly 'automotive,' with cars, trucks, buses, of very frequent appearance; even the helicopter, in my childhood, was more commonly called an 'autogiro,' being then in the *experimental* stage.

A friend used to say of the artist: He makes his ivory tower out of the horn of Behemoth.

A riddle and a joke from childhood. If I put them down at all it had better be without apology.

What goes in hard and comes out soft? The answer: chewing gum. If you answered otherwise, you had a dirty mind.

My father smokes through his ass. How do you know? I saw the nicotine stains in his underwear.

I noted down these identifications of oral and genital, oral and anal, not merely because they 'happened to come to mind,' but because there was a perfectly plain relation between them and the meaning of 'horn'—which I seem to have suppressed immediately. The phrase from Dante is a possible link. And I remember the vague idea appearing before me while I was writing, of 'an ivory cigarette holder,' but this never really achieved the status of a memory. There is one very tenuous yet rather precise constatation of all this imagery, though, in some lines I wrote six years ago.

> It is night
> In the palace, and the Minotaur,
> Our janitor, is smoking in the cellar,
> Sitting alone among turds and bones and dottle.
> To him, enter the naked Athenian youths and maidens,
> —*Seven Macabre Songs*, Nr. 5, "Bluebeard's Wife."

Those songs were commissioned by a composer (how nice if
he had put in a horn accompaniment, but no), they proceed
mostly by the relations of sex-death-filth-lameness, and a
couple of other images from them seem relevant to the
thoughts of the past couple of days: "My death with a nail
in his foot . . . carried a long tooth for a cane." In the pas-
sage quoted above, "dottle" makes it clear that the Minotaur
smoked a pipe, which is a kind of horn, and he is associated
with "turds and bones" as well. In the story of Theseus the
sacrificed youths and maidens attracted me erotically, and the
image of them would accompany masturbation which, by the
way, I regarded with a religious guilt and seriousness, my
secret word for it being, of all words in the world, 'worship.'
My father once caught me at it, and said he would kill me
if it ever happened again; that may be why, in the poem,
when "moms and dads are shrunken into sleep," Bluebeard's
wife expresses a strange wish,

> That I may beard him and unlock the door
> Where the Athenian adolescents fell,
> And find his soul, maybe, and crack it like an egg.

The operations of the ucs., however, are sometimes ridicu-
lously clear. Here is an instance, for relief. While I have been
writing these notes which so often express me as having been
in childhood on the horns of a dilemma between birth and
shit, my wife's time has about come but she still hasn't had
the baby. Last night I was playing a record given me by a
friend (a psychiatrist) years ago, which for some reason I
had never bothered to play before. What is that? asks M.
And I, That? O, that's Schütz, *The Nativity*. Given the ob-
stinacy of the real world, that's a remarkably well-composed
expression of dilemma, wish, megalomaniac phantasy.

Unicorn and Minotaur. The one a beautiful, harmonious (one-horned) nature associated with virginity and white magic (healing, purifying of waters by his horn), who unhappily doesn't happen to exist; the other a double-natured bully boy with two horns, a crazy mixed-up kid you might say, associated with darkness, dirt, secrecy, shame, and death, his mother's fault (Minos was merely shocked at the whole affair), who is kept in an ingeniously designed cellar on a diet of children. . . . Well, isn't that nice?

True, however, that the Minotaur exists no more than the Unicorn does. Meaning to say, maybe, that all this agreeable-disagreeable work of interpretation and memory refers not to a fictive and a real character, but to a couple of fictive ones, the latter of whom has more of an apparent claim to reality only because he is somewhat more secret than the former.

Repeatedly during the past few days I have imagined myself as another reader, and heard this other reader saying, "This is the stupidest book I've ever read, this is plain silly," and so on. Probably, on the other hand, he is quite right, this other reader who is also myself; and probably, again, he expresses my resentment against looking into my life and trying to say how it looks. Toward this other reader who is also in my life I feel a good deal of defensive resentment and hostility, too; I feel a necessity to explain to him, to defend what I am doing, to ask him questions.

But I might better begin by sympathizing with him a little. Admitted (I might say), I have drawn you into what has every chance of being some very elaborate con-game, artistic (and repulsive) in its very uselessness: You might be cheated, without my profiting by it. For one thing, you are constantly asked to believe—or not even asked, your belief is simply assumed—that I am telling, if not the truth, what appears to me to be the truth; that when I say something just came into my mind and surprised me, I really mean just that, when I say I have just remembered I mean I really have just remembered, and so on. Even granted so much, and it's a great deal, I take a great deal more: You are required to believe, or pretend to believe, along with me, that our daily reality is somehow expressive, symbolic, transpicuous, in the way that dreams are (or are by some said to be), that art works are similarly comparable to dreams, that my so-called memories refer to my real past, and not to something I have conveniently made up on the instant to suit a theory or, less than a theory, an ad hoc resemblance. You have to put up with numerous indelicate remarks, a really puerile obsession with excrement and anecdotes referring to infantile theories of anal birth; in addition to which you are always in some doubt whether I believe in all this, or whether I am simply conforming myself fictively and academically to what I have read (as Groddeck said to an early analyst, "You talk a great deal about anality, but have you yourself ever inspected an anus?"). You are asked to credit that my wild synecdochic leaping from likeness to likeness, resulting in what might be called a poetic or imagist sorites, is a valid method for apprehending the truth of a matter. And finally, you must have been asking yourself for some time, if you have been patient enough to read so far, Where does this end? How can it end? Instead of clarifying the writer's character, it must simply dissolve in dialectic the idea of character as a category. The details of any human life are innumerable: Is the fellow then going to remember everything? And what if he did? Dear Reader. Dear Me!

Perhaps the most forceful objection of all is missing from that catalogue; it is that such an account can never come to an end, not merely in the temporal sense, but ideally: You will never be in a position to put down the results in some simple tabulation or summary or syndrome.

It occurs to me, however, that if this is so it is so because the writer is, however precariously, sane. The definition of sanity used here is a simple one, and homemade: If you read through some taxonomical study of mental illness, of the neuroses and psychoses, and identify, say, 90 per cent of the forms described with yourself, you are sane. For sanity is a balance of insanities, an unstable balance at that. But if, on reading such descriptions, you keep saying, Well, anyhow, I don't have *that*, you had probably best be off to the couch at once.

This is therefore a character analysis, and, as such, quite probably interminable as Freud suggests.

1 VIII

Now it is to me to ask the Reader some questions about what we are doing here. The essential questions are put very concisely, not by me:

> Tell me, where all past yeares are,
>   Or who cleft the Divels foot? (the turtle's foot).

I shall try first to expand and vary these questions. How do you distinguish waking life from dreaming with respect to your past? Where is that past? Who are you, and what happens when you try to say so? (I recommend, in this connexion, a brilliant analysis by Nigel Dennis, in the Preface to his *Two Plays and a Preface*: he decides you are your name, nothing more.) In what sense can your life be said to belong to you, to be your possession?

Again, what is Original Sin, the secret wound of the turtle, the *vulnera naturae*—however you express it, what went wrong at the beginning, before the beginning? Can you ever find it, make it well again?

Dear Reader, poor Reader, poor dear. The real past is not distinguished from the past of dreams by chronological and consequential ordering. If you try to do that, you get only the ultimate poverty of your life, your progression through an abstract form laid down for you by civilization, something having about as much interest, as much life, as an entry in *Who's Who* (title sounding very like an owl). Whereas if you try to remember your life, if you look for its ultimate richness, chronology for the most part vanishes, the scheme breaks down; either there is something else, or there is nothing.

Consider. First we were nothing. Now we are something. After a little we shall be nothing again. The interval, while we are something, seems immensely important, we agonize over it terribly, even if some wise person soothes us by setting our toothache in a perspective of light-years, galaxies, spiral nebulae, the toothache continues to hurt as though it had not heard. Toothaches can sometimes be dealt with by dentists, but never by philosophers. Life is very short, a brief instant of light; but every instant of it may contain all eternity.

We began in wet and darkness, and even into the dry light we brought that wet and darkness. So much of what we learned, perhaps the essential forms of all we ever learn, belong back there, a learning without understanding that conditions our later understanding . . . of everything. What is said here of the individual consciousness may be said also of historical consciousness, civilization, the written and monumental record; it defines itself continuously with the darkness that it is not, or that it says it is not. Reason rooted in what is not reason, history in what is not history, mind in what is not mind.

There have been developed, to help us through all this, immensely impressive disciplines, which mostly are related to our activities as tennis courts are related to playing tennis. But the dialectical relation still holds: The existence of tennis courts is also a guarantee of the existence of undefined spaces

that are not tennis courts, and where tennis playing is un-
thinkable. The object of exploration is to find what is think-
able in those immensities. But very few of us are explorers,
and even those few are explorers perhaps only for a few min-
utes during their lives; for the rest, and for the most part, the
parameters of experience are synonymous with the experiences
possible to be had.

This is a simple enough thing, and if it
looks cryptic that is only because I have been trying to say it
with the greatest generality.

A child who grows up to be a tennis player does so in part
because tennis playing exists, has been invented. Something
in his own nature responds to the situation, but now we are
talking about the situation itself, prior to his individuality,
and to which his individuality conforms itself, through which,
in a limited way, his being expresses itself. This child, when
he grows up, does not revolt against the rules of tennis.
(Understood that the rules of tennis may change many times;
but the game at any given instant is regarded by the players
as eternal, and unaffected by time.)

A child who grows up to be an artist likewise does so in part
because art exists. Its rules are sometimes as clear as those of
tennis, more often not. But because art contains, not only
the spirit of the game, which it does just as tennis does, but
something more, something other, a quite different spirit per-
haps opposed to the first, this child, when he grows up, may
have to contemplate the existence of a situation of art very
different from what he learned, what the wise claim to be the
situation, &c. As an artist, he is like a crooked gambler who
turns up with his marked cards and loaded dice only to find
out he is entered in the six-day bike race; he will be breathless
before he can rest on the seventh day.

If this or something like it happens to the child he may be compelled to consider his situation from the beginning, or from as near the beginning as he is able to get. His techniques for doing this are going to be somewhat curious, being at the same time derivative and homemade. And he will have to get along as well as he can with the ghostly company of the understanding that his results may be nil, or silly, or irrelevant. But he must adventure to be silly, if only because everything that is sane, sensible, and accepted, now looks to him mediocre, stupidly safe, an evasion, and finally impossible.

To return now to this child's situation. The situation of literature, the 'problem' of literature, at the present moment in America is widely discussed in the most superficial way, not only without understanding but also in a confined space where no understanding can possibly emerge. The questions, for example, of 'high culture' vs. 'mass culture,' of 'academic' vs. 'beat' (or whatever), of 'form' vs. 'content,' 'form' vs. 'freedom,' 'decorum' vs. 'passion,' are of no interest to the maker because they are asked in a realm which does not concern itself with the real being of art at all; the questioners tacitly assume that all that has been settled; a plague on both their houses.

This situation could stand some pages of illustration and comment. But I do not want to be drawn into that discussion more than is necessary for the purpose of my inquiry, which began as the study of my inadequacy, incapacity, not theirs. But one thing may be said to relate the two areas. I was complaining, or my Reader was, a while back, that an investigation such as this one could never end, either temporally or in a clearly understood and simply apprehensible result. But what inquiry ever does end, especially with reference to art? The learned continue during long and distinguished careers on what appears to be the implicit faith that problems are solved and put away, though the problems of art are solved only in works, and the appearance of a solution otherwhere soon reveals itself as existing only to generate new problems, or the same problems over again. "What has concluded," asked Benjamin Paul Blood, "that we should conclude something about it?" Justice Holmes gave an even glummer expression to the same thought: "Continuity with the past is not a duty," he said, "only a necessity."

It is not my childhood that I seek, but the childhood of my art. As much as to say, Mommy, where do images come from?

It may be that to this phantastic question I have turned up only phantastic answers, symbolic equations and apparent transformations which really express only identities, statements impossible to be distinguished from tautologies, in which what looks to be a predicate and therefore a new result turns out to be only a reiteration of the subject. At the same time, though, certain prospective consistencies have emerged, which I can put down in a simplified, perhaps oversimplified, way, and with no pretense that the order of the summary is other than arbitrary.

1. The pond as birthplace and deathplace, the liquid mother and mirror whence beautiful and terrible forms arise, and whereto they return.

2. Artefacts and representations, for example the portrait of my sister and myself, the Rodin statue and others, the poems I have written about.

3. *Seeing*, as the mediator between the pond and the art work. Seeing as forbidden and punishable, seeing protested to

be innocent. Photography as the antithesis (guilty) of writing (innocent), and the subsequent revelation that all I said about photography had to be applied word for word to writing as well.

I remember a passage in Valéry where he talks about Nature's always constructing her solid forms out of liquids (*Les Coquilles*). It seems as though I have been saying, in a confused and 'historical' way, that art is the secret (holy, forbidden) observation of this process and its reverse, having to do with metamorphosis and the relation, or identity, of the evanescent with the enduring; that the model for this process is sexual and generative, so that one approaches it always with equal fascination and fear, as Milton approached the Spirit that

> from the first
> Wast present, and with mighty wings outspread
> Dove-like satst brooding on the vast Abyss
> And madst it pregnant,

in a passage that began with Man's first disobedience, and the fruit of that forbidden tree, &c.

Now the antithesis I tried to set up between photography and writing may be seen in other terms as well: science (knowing) and art (making). Or: memory and imagination. (I can see now a passionate protestation of innocence, a plea for innocence, in Blake's "Imagination is the Divine Vision. . . . Imagination has nothing to do with Memory.") I have several times noted the division in this writing between the imaginative weaving of connexions, which I characterized by turns as innocent (harmless) and superficial, and the associations to individual memory, which invariably turned out to be not innocent at all, rather dirty and furtive, as well as somewhat inert and without valency.

Now the opposition between imagination and memory (which I have read in other writers, Stendhal for one, Wilson Knight for another) has always puzzled me: How could it be true? Whence could imagination come, if not from memory? And I felt sometimes rather treacherous to poetry in questioning thus. But at the same time I may have been watching out for a synthesis of the two, a harmony of science and poetry, knowing and making, and I remember where I found such a harmony in the writing of a scientist which I gave to my students at the beginning of a course in poetry and poetics as "an example of what I mean by the essentially poetic." The scientist was Sir Charles Sherrington, and the passage I mean comes from his book *Man on His Nature*. Now I had read this book before, and no note in my copy indicates I was especially attracted to one particular place in it, but when I came across part of a chapter reprinted as a memorial in *Scientific American* I was amazed at its grandeur, its brilliance, its poetry, which gave me the sense that I was, under the guidance of this very wise man, penetrating deep into the secrets of Nature. This writing took for its subject the making of the eye, and its constantly iterated metaphor, used both for likeness and difference, said that the eye was a camera.

The reasons for my excitement over Sherrington's essay can clearly not have been scientific; like many poets, I read a good deal of science, and, like most of the poets who do, I do not read it for the sake of science but rather for the sake of metaphor. I shall copy out some of Sherrington's metaphors and descriptions, including many that I copied out at the time along with some others.

"The likeness (of the eye) to an optical camera is plain beyond seeking." If a craftsman making a camera were "told to relinquish wood and metal and glass and to use instead some albumen, salt and water, he certainly would not proceed even to begin." "Water is the great menstruum of 'life.' It makes life possible." "The eye-ball is a little camera." The adjustment of the lens to more and less light in a camera "is made by the observer working the instrument. In the eye this adjustment is automatic, worked by the image itself!"

Particularly striking to me: "all this making of the eye which *will* see in the light is carried out in the dark. It is a preparing in darkness for use in light."

And: "This living glass-clear sheet is covered with a layer of tear-water constantly renewed. This tear-water has the special chemical power of killing germs which might inflame the eye. This glass-clear bit of skin has only one of the four-fold set of the skin-senses; its touch is always 'pain,' for it should *not* be touched."

Associations cluster about that in particular. "The pride of life and the lust of the eye." *King Lear,* which continually claims that eyes were made for weeping, not for seeing; or for seeing only in order to weep, and not for the sake of intellect and advantage. Cordelia calls sight "this most precious square of sense." Empson: "It is the two / Most exquisite surfaces of knowledge can / Get clap (the other is the eye)."

There is much more I might quote from Sherrington, but I shall add only this one telling sentence at this moment: "And the whole structure, with its prescience and all its efficiency, is produced by and out of specks of granular slime arranging themselves as of their own accord in sheets and layers, and acting seemingly on an agreed plan."

He himself, I see, compares the account to fiction: "It all sounds an unskilful overstated tale which challenges belief."

Subjecting, according to the method of my book, this scientifically accurate and imaginatively convincing story to association with my imagery, working on the premise that its combination with imagery intrinsic to my poetry is what gave it so great a power over my thought, I have to relate it at once to the pond, to seeing, to photography, and to art. Indeed, eye and pond were earlier related in a poem where I said "the clear lake of the eye," eye, pond, and camera were put together in another:

> There is a threshold, that meniscus where
> The strider walks on drowning waters, or
> That tense, curved membrane of the camera's lens
> Which darkness holds against the battering light
> And the distracted drumming of the world's
> Importunate plenty. . . .
>
> *Runes,* XIV

(Those lines were written before my second reading of Sherrington, though not certainly before the first.)

If these observations are, as I said earlier, like that Game of the Novel I described some time ago, then I ought to have added that I am like the novelist who, though he didn't know the trick, was protected by his professional vanity. That is, I tend to respond from my poems rather than from my life, example of a division frequently remarked on during the past weeks. But surely there is some relation. And it would be interesting to be able to say something of what it is.

I do want to get back to the passage from Sherrington, which seems to have something more to say than I have been able to elicit so far. But first, here is a curious instance of—well, of I don't know exactly what.

Before sleep, reading a few pages of a detective story, I had the idea of putting down a phrase at random, just to see if it would determine my dream in any apparent way. But I don't know if I had the idea before hitting on the phrase, or whether I had just seen the phrase which so struck me as to give the idea. Anyhow, the phrase said that some Negroes being questioned by the police were "African war masks in the dead white light." And then I dreamed of someone "erecting a statue to Sanders of the River, Mr Commissioner Sanders." However you put the cause and effect relation, the correspondence is remarkably close. This Sanders is a fictional character about whom Edgar Wallace wrote some of his best stories, he appealed to me maybe by being a sort of low-grade melodramatic replica of Conrad's Marlow, my favorite person in fiction. Sanders was a policeman, white, for a colonial district in Africa. In the dream a statue is being put up, therefore he is dead (dead white, says the phrase I copied down), and the statue is the counterpart of the African war masks, too.

On putting that down I am all at once as though struck dumb, paralyzed with unwillingness to look any further, either into that dream or into the complex represented by the eye, the camera, the pond. I shall have to try, but I keep saying not now, and think I have a fair idea what it is I am so ashamed of.

THREE DREAMS ON THE SAME THEME

1. In a card game, I get the ace of spades; a second card, also face down, is the ace of clubs. I am pleased, until the game turns out to be a new form of rummy rather than poker, so that I have to discard one of the aces.

2. A large structure somewhat resembling the Polo Grounds (ramps, a green shedlike roof) is on fire. Wandering about, I realize that my family (wife and child) are upstairs, in a wing that has not yet caught fire, but that if I go up to warn them I will probably be trapped there as the fire spreads, as indeed it now begins to do.

3. On an ocean liner in trouble, possibly sinking, possibly on fire. I am with my father on the lower deck at the stern; above us, at the rail, is my mother. My father is sick, and cannot move. Then the ship is fixed, we go faster, with much more vibration, everyone smiles. I go forward and have a

drink, observing that I can look the whole length of the deck aft, which is practically deserted. Then I go back amidships and have another. While I am paying for this second drink, which is very expensive ($1.90) and involves also the purchase of a chocolate bar from a pack containing two, and a piece of sugar, a waitress comes with five dollars and some silver in change for the first drink, though I have not paid for it.

The three dreams have in common the offer of alternatives. I may have one ace at the expense of the other; my safety at the expense of my family's; stay with my father or go to my mother. The 'one out of two' theme is reiterated in the chocolate bars and drinks of the third dream. In the first dream I am merely disappointed, in the second I am a coward but preserved from the demonstration by the fire which already takes away the power of choice; in the third dream I am liberated from all responsibility by others (the ship's officers, who in the dream rather sarcastically assure the passengers that there is no longer any danger).

Association to 2. The Heiji-Monogatari Roll (Burning of the San-Jo Palace) in the Boston Museum. This roll is a narrative, and perhaps is there to suggest in the first place that the three dreams have to be read as three stages in one story.

Nose to the grindstone, teeth clenched, tongue firmly in cheek, be as silly as seems necessary. "Very expensive ($1.90)" associates itself with the Mercedes Benz 190 SL, which I have sometimes had dreamy thoughts about buying (not very serious). Mercedes Benz reverses in the initials Boston Museum, commonly BM (with the usual associations) or BMFA (with the usual associations). On thinking this, I began to ask whether SL didn't also appear elsewhere in the dreams, and presently found it very close indeed, in the dollar sign, $, a compound of S and l.

In the first dream, at the beginning, I am playing stud poker (my game), but it turns into rummy (my father's game), to my disadvantage; for if rummy could have the same format as, say, seven-card stud, it is clearly no good to be dealt two aces at once, since you have to throw one back (making the other almost worthless). My father played gin rummy habitually. I drink gin habitually. Yesterday I forgot to buy gin; a friend and I drank rum instead. He concocted a new drink (new form of rummy), using orange juice and, for a not very good joke, maple syrup; I mentioned that rum and maple syrup were traditionally connected (rum and molasses), and may add now that both are connected also with the slave trade (two black aces, black as the ace of spades, &c.; also *slave*). Association: a moment's phantastic thought yesterday that the new baby would be a Negro; how embarrassed I would be.

This is the point of difficulty at which I stopped seven days ago: that the analysis was compelling me to talk about Negroes and blackness, which I violently and sullenly resisted doing on the apparent ground that while 'I myself' am liberal my ucs. is pretty clearly not.

8 VIII

I note also that my shame about not continuing with this for seven days expressed itself first in a refusal to date the first page of today's writing; second, in the equal and opposite impulse that finally gave the show away by 'internal evidence' ("seven days ago"), even making a mistake in order to bring in the thematic "seven," for it was really but six days ago.

A memory associated with "at the rail" and "my mother" (3). The home movie, where Mother pretended to be making love to another man, was made on an ocean liner. That dates it to my seventh year, when we went to France on the *Aquitania*. But also to my seventeenth, when we returned on the *Normandie* and I tried to make love to a girl rather older than myself, was doing quite well until we went as far "forward" as we could, looking "the whole length of the deck aft" which was "practically deserted"; I opened a door forward then to an open verandah beneath and parallel with the bridge—and was nearly swept overboard by the wind; which put a stop to any further advances that evening, as we were both rather shaken. Were these memories brought up by the mere mention of seven? We have so far "seven days ago," "seven-card stud," and implicitly that gin rummy is played with seven cards; those boat trips were in 1927 and 1937 respectively. Would ingenuity press so far as to say that the "five dollars and some silver" + $1.90 = $7.00, making the some silver amount to twenty cents or two dimes? I horrify myself. But in another card game, played in boyhood, where one bet a dime, you could split the first two cards if they were the same, bet double, and play each hand separately; that game, of course, was *black*jack (or twenty-one = 3×7).

But I see that my ingenuity is too enthusiastic to add right. It would be one dime, and I have again made an error comparable to the mismemory about the Wandering Jew, where I said he slapped Christ and meant spit instead of slap.

On the other hand, the spider's web of association doesn't let go so easily. For now, combining the two errors and taking, so to say, the compound interest on them, we have two other card games from early life: Spit in the Ocean, and Slap or Snap (associated with Stripjack Naked, associated with Strip Poker). (Christ and the self identified by G. M. Hopkins: "I am all at once what Christ is, since he was what I am, and / This Jack, joke, poor potsherd, patch, matchwood, immortal diamond, / Is immortal diamond." "That Nature is a Heraclitean Fire, and Of the Comfort of The Resurrection.") "Thou shalt have more / Than two tens to a score" (*King Lear*). 'Jack' is also a picture card; elsewhere, and elsewhere in Hopkins, too, you have "Christ the king." Diamond is another card word.

This is all so remote and complicated and tenuous I am tempted to throw it away for absurd. Having got so far, though, I add the suddenly returned memory of a dream from a few nights ago: a father and a son, the first venerable, the second twenty years less venerable, something like seventy and fifty. The son was planning to kill the father, or possibly the father was planning to kill the son. But then it all turned into a joke, and they laughed together about it. They were both

Italians. Beatrice was mentioned. On waking I said that this
dream was unnarratable.

All this may simply be an evasion of Negroes and blackness.
A long time ago, near the beginning of these notes I men-
tioned an identification of Negro with feces, and said I had
been too embarrassed to record the dream that gave it me.
Not true. It is recorded in my Notebooks for 18 III 63, and I
repeat it, with its related comment, here.

Following R into town, we go by a steep way which turns
into a swamp full of rotting logs. He leaps lightly across and
turns to help me, but I say I can make it but want to go
slowly. Later, I am walking alone on the other road into
town; it is night. I overtake a Negro, who wants to be sure this
is the easy road; I am able to reassure him, and we proceed
together. I realize that he is just as frightened as I am.

Concerning this I wrote at that time: "I remember thinking
several times recently how the problem for the Negro in
America is tragically related to the white man's problem with
his own feces, hence could never be resolved by reasonable
discussion, law, &c. And I made up the slogan which said that
our question was not integrate or segregate, but integrate or
disintegrate.

"The basis for my strange assertion concerning the Negro
might be found in the rule of life which seems to say, in the
South, that the Negro's place is always at the back, at the back
of the bus, the back door of the house, the back of town.
The servant's quarters, of course, gain symbolic force of this
kind by being quite literally the place whence garbage is dis-
posed." (Hindquarters; hind = servant, slave.)

A confused, or condensed, memory of a much earlier dream about a Negro, amounting in affect to a terrified religious revelation. One memory says that in this dream a Negro was killed and hung upside down on a butcher's hook in a refrigerated room; another memory says that a giant Negro, naked to the waste,* had done the killing and hung the flayed corpse (white?) on a hook, and now came at me with a cleaver. Waking, I thought first, What a terrible man that Negro is, and, immediately after, There was no Negro, there was only yourself; you were the Negro, the corpse, the murderer; probably you provided the hook and the refrigeration as well.

Now I am well aware of my temptation to ease off the pressure by referring to poems instead of memories; on the other hand, the poems do frequently put together my iterative imagery in a somewhat illuminating way, so that I cannot resist entering the following rich combination, which oddly enough took me several minutes to find; I had to look through three of my own books.

The poem is called "A Picture," and describes a newspaper photograph of white people running down a street, "hunting down a Negro, according to the caption." The white people are metaphorically seen as cattle headed for the slaughterhouse, with "the serious patience of animals / Driven through a gate by some / Urgency out of the camera's range," and, in an ironic conclusion, as "Obedient, it might be, to the Negro, / Who was not caught by the camera," &c. Segregation, butchery, seeing, the camera, are put together with a mocking expression of religious feeling: the faces of the whites "Expressed a religion of running," and so on.

But perhaps all this is no more than to say I am about what I am about, my concerns at one time are my

* I have to leave 'waste' for 'waist' as appropriate; I almost never misspell words.

concerns at another time. . . . Still, what the poem tries to say is something like this: The camera is false art, one cannot tell what these people are doing except by means of a caption, after one is told one doesn't want to believe that people actually do anything like that, and the camera leaves out the very object of all this senseless activity, that is, presents an incomplete view of reality. Therefore the white people who appear in the picture are "caught by the camera," it 'took' them in the sense of 'took them in,' while the Negro victim, however he may have suffered, was at any rate not the victim of their illusions, which (the poem did not explicitly add) show the world as 'black and white.'

Another poem, arbitrarily placed next to that one, is also about newspapers and relates the Negro question to sexual questions by speaking of "the segregated photographs / Of the girls that marry and the men that die." I remember thinking that another example of segregation in our society appears in the signs Men and Women, but that no one crusades for integration here. And, a funny rider to that one, M confessed to being embarrassed while we were in the South by something that had never bothered her, or even occurred to her, before: that when you went to the Laundromat you naturally 'segregated' the white clothes and the colored.

Bathrooms, washing, keeping clean (being 'white' in the sense of pure), food (the butchered corpses), killing and being killed, ritual sacrifice, clean clothing, sexual relations, privacy (as in 'privy'), all run together with (cannot be segregated from) the dream about defecation and dirt that began this cluster of associated images.

Offhand, I have very few memories of Negroes, have known very few. Yet it appears to me as though the Negro people exemplify some of my worst fears and most shameful secret thoughts. It horrifies me to have to discuss the subject, because consciously I want to see our society integrated (instead of destroyed), regard American treatment of Negroes, both in North and South, as shameful (using, I see, the same word about the public as about the private motif) and absurd. But if I do not discuss the subject, I fail at what so far is the nearest to an ultimate confrontation these notes have presented, and so I fail at their object. So discuss, and don't be so timid.

The statement, whether true or not, that "I have very few memories of Negroes," &c., immediately offers a reason for their possibly symbolizing something very nasty, mean, and secret in myself. What one doesn't know is a good territory for the growth of phantasies. And the more you don't know something, the more reason you find for not getting to know; avoidance itself becomes a motive for avoidance. The Negro is 'strange' and 'dark.' In a characteristic metaphor, he is a photographic negative of the white man, and allegorically is victimized by being made to represent evil in all contests of black and white (even ambiguously and ironically, as in such a contest represented on the stern of the vessel in Melville's *Benito Cereno*).

Like any number of well-intentioned white people, I am ill at ease with Negroes. First, because I am aware that as a white I owe them something; they represent my bad conscience. Second, because I know that they are aware of this, hence have the power of seeing through my politeness, amiableness, and self-consciousness about these. I do not like for people to be in a position which allows them to see more irony in life than I am able to (which is, after all, a fair lot). Third, because they so often appear as servants, and the position of servant is always a position of immense power, hence a threat (just as the Devil characteristically appears as a servant). It goes with this that I disliked and rather feared servants in childhood (few if any of these were colored), and I remind myself that a child's relation with the parents' servants is an extremely precarious one; if they are below the parents they are nevertheless above the children; their power to love or withhold love, or even to punish, threaten, be cruel or mean or unfair, is perhaps not greater than that of the parents but is surely more continuous and constantly present—and may effectively be greater, at that. The relation is ambiguous, because the child has a power too, the power of telling on the servant, and this is an economic power connected with shame; that is, if you got the maid fired (and especially during the Depression) you would have to feel that you had unintentionally produced an effect disproportionate to the cause, and that you had been a sneak. Also, servants always knew what you were doing, and even when they couldn't or were disinclined to punish you for it, they might laugh at you, which is worse.

In a more secret set of notions, Negroes smell different, they represent poverty, hence filth, and they are entitled to represent 'envy from the depths,' or the fear of revolution; again they are my bad conscience about being white (clean) which relates to my boyhood bad conscience about being rich. All this was carried on during College, too, where I was ashamed of being rich, where ever so many people said, as it was fashionable to do then, that the son of rich parents could never be a poet. Easy to see why I respond with unquestioning assent to the Freudian equation between money and feces, it is a sorites involving an economic relation of servant and master, the unconscious identification of poverty with filth with 'the depths,' that is, the sexual and excretory arrangements of the body. Which may be why my few meetings with Negroes are infected by my self-consciousness and my awareness of their knowledge of it, by my masochistic wish to see myself as a victim, expressing itself in attitude as my putting myself out to be pleasant, &c.: "See how well I am behaving, see how good (what a good boy) am I!"

It seems extremely likely that the rich red inside of the Negro's mouth, with its very white teeth, shown in laughter, is my secret image for the female genital. But I have no memory to go with that.

Oops, I'm afraid that is not quite so.

> Little Jack Horner
> Sat in a corner
> * * *
> He stuck in his thumb
> And pulled out a plum
> And said what a good boy am I!

This relates to the Negro by means of my earliest memory. A little boy fell off his tricycle on the sidewalk. He bled from the mouth. "Grandma," I cried, running into the house, "there are plums coming out of his mouth." Stewed plums, stewed prunes, early aversions, no wonder at it. Additional relations: the imagery about horns, minotaur, unicorn, &c., a few days ago; and what has been said this morning about 'Jack.' Probably I once was little Jack Horner, and now I am Big Jack Horner, but not out of trouble even so. (Jack = the penis, jack off = jerk off.)

The missing line, at least in English versions, is "Eating a Christmas pie." I don't respond to that, maybe we had a different line there. But I had this rime confused with Miss Muffet "eating some curds and whey" for a moment while I was writing out the verses; the spider strikes again. Still, the

Christmas pie repeats the connexion between Jack and Christ made earlier today; and an odd memory attaches itself to that: a medieval joke about a housewife raped by a priest behind the altar; in revenge she bakes him a pie to give to his bishop, the pie is full of shit. This is from Salimbene's chronicle, translated by Coulton as *From St. Francis to Dante*, but the anecdote itself is left in Latin in an appendix prefaced with a paragraph of Coulton's more classical Latin beginning "*Vix credibile est. . . .*" (So I do know Latin after all, this memory claims, and adds to 'Latin as a dead language, a religious language, a language of the dead' the news that Latin is also a language in which one tells dirty stories.) Does this Italian story have any affinity for the dream of the Italian father and son? Beyond the mention of 'Beatrice,' relating to 'Dante' in the title of the book, there is one: When the boy Salimbene (= Jump into good, his religious name) proposes to take Holy Orders, his given name being then Ognibene (= All good), his father says to him roughly, "Why do you want to go with them pants-pissers (quos pissin-tunicas)?"

Have I remembered those items for a couple of dozen years because I studied Salimbene with ———, whose homosexual proclivities (I was his confidante, not his partner) formed the subject of one of my early stories, in which he killed himself, and who in fact killed himself by the same means (chemical) ten years later? And does that relate to telling on servants ("that you had unintentionally produced an effect disproportionate to the cause, and that you had been a sneak")? Does fiction, then, represent, in addition to everything else it represents, the betrayal of others, a once-successful move of aggression against another person, which I ambiguously hope and fear to repeat? I fear this analysis, remote as are the connexions by which I come to this point, has a good deal to support it.

8 VIII

In notes about the composition of another story, "Yore," I was able to see that M's suffering at that time had a good deal of an immediate nature to do with my being able to produce easily this most distant and cruel of my short stories. Some of the first of my best poems were done while M was enduring a fairly difficult miscarriage. I remember having had many times in the past years the thought that "When my father dies I shall be able to write fiction." The original power of the poet is said to be the power to bless or curse, and I kept in mind for many years the situation of a king of Ulster and Connaught (my father?) who could not be cursed because his name would not scan in any known meter (Briffault, *The Mothers*). And I have often had it in mind (a) that these notes are being written during the last weeks of M's pregnancy (as though in competition to produce) and (b) that I think of this writing as specifically bridging the interim between my father's death and the birth of the new baby, as though the one's going out of the world had to be balanced against the other's coming into it.

These reflexions bring us round *da capo* to the three dreams, or triple dream, that began this morning's meditation. I can't see by any means all about them, or very deeply into them, but it may be worth putting down all the same the little more I can see.

The two aces, of which one must be given back, refer to my father's dying as though this made possible the birth of the child. But my son, like my father, is named David, and the second reference of the dream is to a fear that somehow my son will be taken in exchange for the new baby. On this phantasy, see the similar one about King David at II Samuel 12-13; also 18 ("And it came to pass on the seventh day, that the child died" = the seven days' intermittence in this writing, during which I frequently excused myself by saying that it was time for the baby to be born, I couldn't concentrate, and so on).

The idea that I might have remembered that anecdote is repugnant as it is far-fetched. And yet possible: Those stories in the Bible belong deeply and terribly to my childhood, hence also to my poems, which often refer to them; and I have studied them in adult life as well. I may add that at my father's death my uncle, who by mere coincidence is named after Nathan the prophet, rebuked me for reducing to a minimum the religious observances at the funeral, which I did on the stated ground that my father in late years told me he did not believe in 'all that.' This was not a lie, and not quite not a lie. What my father did say, asking me a couple of years back if I would go with him to the Temple on Yom Kippur, was something like, "I don't blame you," adding suddenly, "I always hated my father and his religion." He went all the same, though certainly not to the sort of orthodox rite my uncle was proposing.

But I shan't name a new boy Solomon.

The second dream may express again the wish that my wife and the new baby may die, in order that I may not be 'trapped.' The dream makes me responsible for warning them, then reassures me by saying they are already beyond help (the fire already has begun to spread), which, after all, is allegorically true: I cannot help her have the child (or, ironically, I have already done all I can, done my part, &c.).

The third dream expresses a similar helplessness in disaster, a similar release from responsibility. The ship's officers are the doctors who attended my father, they 'did everything possible,' of course, and he died. ("All was holy, all was honorable.") "The ship is fixed, we go faster, with much more vibration, everyone smiles." This refers to something I frequently observed during my father's illness. The family is utterly helpless, all they can do is 'behave beautifully.' But they have to give every practical recourse over to the doctors (ship's officers), and on the doctors' professional assurances everyone yields over and over again to a hysterical optimism, even though "we go faster," that is, toward my father's death, his spasms of suffering ("much more vibration"), but everyone smiles. And I employ this excuse in the dream so as not to stay with my father *and* not comfort my mother but go off to have a drink instead. This drinking is associated with money, great expense, but also with the purchase of a sports car and the unexpected receipt of money (the five dollars and some silver) where I should have been paying out money for my pleasure; perhaps alluding to a thought of inheriting great wealth from my father's death. This thought, or wish, seems to be clearly fixed in the dream-thoughts although not in reality; there is not much money left, and it goes, of course, to Mother, with the children as residual legatees. It was often a relieving thought to me in my guilt over Father's illness, that 'at least' I didn't stand to gain financially by it.

Addenda—8 VIII

A month or so ago, Mother sent me some of my father's belongings, including his razor. I have been using it, and frequently note that I hardly ever cut myself shaving any more, something I formerly did almost every day. I said ingenuously, "Of course, this is a much better razor." Today, however, after writing this morning's notes, I went to shave, and on having the same thought I said, "Or else you don't

need to fear Father any more, because you have his razor."
Whereupon in the next minute I nicked myself half a dozen
times, not seriously, rather as though to say, "Yes, that's all
very well, but it is still dangerous in your hands" (you are a
father, your father survives in you, whatever was threatening
in his nature you have introjected into yourself. His razor
was not an 'injector razor,' by the way. Mine was.).

Imagining the Negro as filth, his mouth as symbolizing the
female genital, it is worth remarking how many correspond-
ences relate those thoughts to the poem about the mud
turtle (a creature of chiefly Southern associations anyhow,
like that turtleish-looking white TV editorialist in Virginia,
who L said was called The Mouth of the South).

                                          The turtle
was seen as black, dark, bearing filth on his back; he comes
up from beneath (the South, the underworld). His teeth are
emphasized, and his claws; red comes in where the toes have
been torn off one foot.

I have tried to keep this inquisition reasonable in tone, cer-
tainly not to hoke it up by getting rhapsodic, or by the usual
literary claim that all this showed great courage on my part,
and *therefore* must be very grand literature. A tone scien-
tifically dispassionate need not prevent my occasionally say-
ing, however, that I would rather not be compelled to write
down these things, would prefer not to look any further into
my nature, and perhaps most of all wish I did not need to
make remarks which an injudicious public might take in the
literal sense as outwardly directed, toward the world; whereas
their sense is symbolic, they are Allegory addressed to the
Intellectual Powers, and as such, according to the vocabulary
of this book, they are determined from within and diagnostic,
if at all, only of the writer himself and the child he was and is.

I happened just then to look down at the Bible, which I had left open after citing the story about David and Bathsheba, Uriah's death, Nathan's denunciation, and the death of the son; well, immediately after, at the beginning of the next chapter, 13, which my eye somehow lit on, begins the story of the incest between the son and daughter of David, the murder of the incestuous son by the agency of his brother Absalom, all which originated the revolution that nearly overthrew the father, who was saved by Absalom's death. The relevance to the theme of these notes is too full to be described. Without going all magical (for "that's how all natural or supernatural stories run"—Yeats), I am inclined to say that the Old Testament is still the most wondrous and terrifyingly deep mysterious book we have; as I said once, the complete program, rule book and score card—though we should not go on making the mistake of having our copies bound in human skin.

A folly persisted in.

9 VIII

The memory of ——'s suicide and its connexion with my story seems to have made possible a distinct advance to a new stage in the perception that the fear of writing fiction, that fear brought up from the very beginning of the study, was also a fear of hurting or killing someone else (as well as, of course, a desire to do this).

That suggests returning to consider the dream that stopped me from writing for a week. That dream was conditioned by a phrase in a piece of fiction, and itself referred to fiction. The phrase "African war masks in the dead white light" somehow 'became' a dream about "erecting a statue to Sanders of the River, Mr Commissioner Sanders."

"Erecting a statue" is redundant, in a way. K and I once discussed statues, and simultaneously came out with the statement, "Statues *are* erections." A fortiori, maybe, Rodin's statue of the embracing couple on the ashtray would be redundant, though of course the erection is 'tastefully' missing. Statues and sex are related at least twice in my poems; both examples think satirically of statues as setting an example to little children, hence as powers behind the dream of history, which I characterized long ago as "a melodrama entitled *The Return of the Repressed*." In some way I have always connected history with aging, have seen the historical process as a "hardening of the arteries," and old people as having hardened into the image of themselves, having become (as in certain Steinberg drawings) statues of themselves.

The idea of statues, connected with the biblical prohibition of graven images, entered into my poetry slowly at first, perhaps seven years ago ("The Statues in the Public Gardens"), but recently with much more frequency and force, so that a third of the poems in my latest book could be grouped together under the general name of *Effigies*, including by analogy with the form and function of statues such metaphorical extensions as photographs, Santa Claus, mannequins in shop windows, snowmen, famous and influential people, and even the unsuccessful heroes turned to stone by the Gorgon's head (this last another phantasy about "history from the point of view of the losers," in which being turned to stone becomes a metaphor for the poet's growing old and defining his character not only in but by his writings).

A strange memory comes in here. For many years, while falling asleep, I would have the feeling that I could not raise my head from the pillow, and the absolute belief that if I did not do this I would die without waking. So with great effort I would tense the muscles of my neck and force my head up, whereon the strange dizziness accompanying the feeling and belief would disappear. The symptom itself left me several years ago, probably on the simple reflexion that what I was experiencing was no more than a conscious perception, on the very edge of consciousness, of what it feels like to go to sleep.

The memory appears at this moment, probably, because it relates rigidity, death, erection, in the 'statuesque' thought of paralysis and helplessness. Statues cannot move, yet they move us by example; they represent impotence and omnipotence simultaneously. In an epigram on this subject, I made Don Juan address the Commander's Statue:

> Dominant marble, neither will I yield!
> The soul endures at one with its election,
> Lover to bed or soldier to the field,
> Your daughter's the cause of this & that erection.

Here is a poem I wrote months before my father's death, on first seeing him in the hospital and learning that he was seriously ill.

GROWING A GHOST

> From the time he knew
> he groomed his hair
> in a grey pompadour
> and made grim his smile
> fitly to represent
> all that would be meant
> When he arrived by growing
> to that great dignity
> nondenominational
> but solemn all the same
> and showing forth a force:

> the stone jaw
> the sharp nose
> the closed lids

> dreaming
> nightmares for all
> who looked their last

9 VIII

looking his best
the ancestral look
in evening clothes
to go underground
and have at last
in his folded hands
the peace of the world

the red clay

As my sister wrote me toward the end, "he looks more like everyman than himself."

So statues seem to represent to me the power of the past, of the dead, specifically a sexual power which is also a fatal power. In the dream, the statue is of a policeman who firmly but fairly metes justice to the Negroes, to whom he is as a father (I seem to remember that in the stories Sanders behaves towards the Negroes as towards children, whether this is explicitly said or not). The Negroes here in question are of course savages, and it may be that the parable expressed in this dream says that the father, or the superego, who controlled the savage black children, or savage impulses, is dead, but the stone image or erection that represents him still dominates the territory he used to control.

Now this writing itself is suspiciously related to that statue; Sanders may equally be my father or my own cold and repressive nature. What I have been writing sometimes commends itself to me as a display of creative potency; while on other days I view it as a fraudulent device for disguising my inability to write fiction, so that it shares with statues the trait of being at once powerful and powerless.

Of course! To write a work of fiction is essentially to tell a story. And to tell a story is to tell a lie, because a lie was a story. So there does exist a prohibition against telling stories, and this prohibition belongs to an early age.

Am I merely fooling myself with verbal tricks (lying to myself, in effect)? Or is there something in it?

Once at school I hid a boy's coat in another locker so that he couldn't find it. When asked, I said I knew nothing about it. But I confessed to my mother the same afternoon, having a tender conscience. It seemed to her a very little thing, but a big one to me; that was perhaps the primordial lie. Or rather, since it represents me as already conscience-stricken, it cannot be; there must have been an earlier one.

Related considerations. I have frequently stressed the factual or veritable nature of my poetry, for example a turtle appears, and I write down the turtle—because that is, after all, what happened. This opens up semantical and linguistic questions demanding sophisticated treatment, but never mind that. I also think of poetry as a matter of listening for what the landscape says to you, a marvelous duplication of the scene in syllables which 'happen to be' appropriate. A certain simplicity is also requisite, even a naïveté; my example for this was that a poet who, seeing a rock in the road, said "There is a rock in the road," is a real poet; the false poet would hoke it up in the transcription.

(The example appears to come from Freud's Rat Man, though, who on seeing a rock in the road removed it lest people should hurt themselves, but then felt compelled to put it back.) I also said to some students of these questions that poetry meant 'keeping your eye on the ball,' but that this must be phrased just so, and not, as a 'modern poet' might do, 'keeping your eyeball on the ball.'

Perhaps this is why writing poetry has never been attended by the kind of moral strain that almost always goes with my writing fiction —because in some way poetry is 'not a lie'? (Also because it is not a duty, that is, makes very little money?)

Equally, that may be why I can write away at this whatever-it-is without great difficulty on most days; because it proposes, with whatever success, to tell the truth.

The first chapter of the novel with Felix Ledger as its hero, a dozen years ago, contained, and indeed was built upon, the telling of a lie and the consequent discussion of lying as a way of life.

Speculation. Sustaining one's own life, sustaining the lie of one's own life, takes so much energy that an additional, a parallel and concurrent lie such as a novel, is rarely possible. Why, then, should it ever have been possible?

A fiction is a projection of real wishes and real fears, real crimes and real punishments, upon persons who do not exist. The resistance to fiction, however, also involves projection: the fear of revealing oneself (what will the others think?), the fear of hurting or destroying others, the fear that the others will revenge themselves.

But there is no magic in all this today. The things I have said, they seem to be only reasons in a world of reasons. It may be that the study nears its end, or, if it can have no end, is readying to be given up.

All through it, I have been aware of the immense solemnity of summer around and above me as I wrote; it informed the thought of the pond as well as much else. So, with a view possibly of the end I shall put down—no 'analysis' here—a poem on this that I wrote yesterday.

Summer's Elegy

Day after day, day after still day,
The summer has begun to pass away.
Starlings at twilight fly clustered and call,
And branches bend, and leaves begin to fall.
The meadow and the orchard grass are mown,
And the meadowlark's house is cut down.

The little lantern bugs have doused their fires,
The swallows sit in rows along the wires.
Berry and grape appear among the flowers
Tangled against the wall in secret bowers,
And cricket now begins to hum the hours
Remaining to the passion's slow procession
Down from the high place and the golden session
Wherein the sun was sacrificed for us.
A failing light, no longer numinous
Now frames the long and solemn afternoons

Where butterflies regret their closed cocoons.
We reach the place unripe, and made to know
As with a sudden knowledge that we go
Away forever, all hope of return
Cut off, hearing the crackle of the burn-
ing blade behind us, and the terminal sound
Of apples dropping on the dry ground.

1. Seeing the movie of *Great Expectations* rerun on TV. Not only rerun, but a continuous performance, so that I am able to tell M what to expect (the opening scene where Pip in the cemetery stumbles against the giant form of Magwich). Moreover, the showing of this scene, which caused such shock among audiences, is prepared, and the shock thus cushioned, by being prefaced with a crude woodcut of the same scene.

Easy to see, among many things clamoring to be seen, how this dream is evoked by what I wrote concerning an inheritance under my father's will (expectations), by the thought of statues (cemetery, the looming up of the convict among stones, a stone among stones), and by the idea of redundancy appearing throughout. We are 'expecting' the baby, and the dream seems to reassure me by making me the expert ("I am able to tell M what to expect"), which is far from the fact. "Rerun," "continuous performance," refer to this writing clearly enough, which is the repetition of the past and shows signs of never being able to come to a conclusion but to be always forced to begin again. "Crude woodcut" belongs in a barber shop; it combines "crew cut" (M cut David's hair yesterday, and he didn't want one) with the funny thing an English barber said to me once when I was directing him in a hesitant effort to cut my hair in that way: "We're getting down awful near the wood, sir." Barbers and dentists belong together for me among life's least agreeable experiences, and the dentist's remark, "We're working awfully near the nerve," is an echo of the barber's but less funny. (Barbers and dentists combined in my short story, earlier referred to, "A Secret Society.")

2. Writing a review. Somehow this is confused with some military exploit, in which I am rebuked by a squadron leader for something. I arrive at what I really want to say just at the bottom of a page, and have to debate whether to squeeze it in or take a new sheet.

"A review" is this writing. Perhaps these two dreams are responsible for my feeling earlier today that I had come to the end of, or would abandon, this examination. In reference to the shipboard dream of a few days ago, with its "$1.90" associated to the sports car 190 SL, "Squadron Leader" was typically abbreviated "S/L." I also, during the intermission of this writing, did write a review that began with a memory of the war.

3. (Seems to be a part of the movie of 1 above.) An Englishman in seventeenth century costume sits at an oak table in a tavern. We learn that he was the first man to find out what is really inside an egg, and that he was honored for this by the King of Spain. I marvel that people got on for so many centuries without knowing what is inside an egg.

2 and 3 together vaguely direct me to a blank in my memory: some probably shameful scene I think I made the night before leaving my squadron of the RAF after finishing my tour. Terribly drunk, I think I made a great fuss before the Wing Commander Flying about my navigator's receiving the Croix de Guerre while I, who drove him around, got nothing. Since

I am supposedly an egghead, the Englishman's finding out what is inside represents the acknowledgment that this secret exists, and my marveling and so on is a pretense that I don't fear the revelation of it. Equally, there is another, more purely symbolic, reading in which the egg and its contents have to do with M and the expected child.

4. Outside the house in the morning three birds sit on a branch: an owl, a starling, a pigeon. They do not fly at my approach, I am able to touch their beaks, and even to carry the pigeon indoors to show M while I look for something to give them to eat.

The first of the dreams reported is also the most immediately fascinating, perhaps only because it concentrates so much of the imagery which has turned up over and over during the past month. Probably the discussion of photography vs. writing is central to any further understanding. For here we have that debate dramatized in the form of a movie made out of a novel. The "opening scene," which "caused such shock among audiences," is a joke about "opening." It is the primal scene of analytic lore, yes, but it is also the opening of the womb and the birth of the child (a photographic study of this, I think in *Life*, did shock the great audience during my adolescence).

Now as to that crude woodcut which "cushioned the shock." It suggests that one learns secret things first from books and pictures, which to a certain extent protects one from the later experienced reality. The puns relating to barbers lead me to infer that the sight of pubic hair is meant. But in the art books from which I first drew my impression of the female sexual parts, pubic hair was generally omitted. "Woodcut" is cipher for a phantasy about castration, because a woman's pubic hair is poetically characterized as a forest (wood) with a cut in it, as for instance "that deep romantic chasm" with its "cedarn cover" in Kubla Khan. "Cushioned" may also be an image for pubic hair, perhaps through an association with "cuisse," sometimes in English writers spelled cushes in the plural (having to do with armor), and it should be noticed that "shock" is used also of hair. The doubly determined relation of barber and dentist is enforced by the thought of castration under the emblem of extracting a tooth.

Probably my thinking of masturbation as "worship" was determined in the first place by the ironic circumstance that naked people both men and women appeared not in amatory paintings so much as in religious paintings, for example "La Chute des Damnées" in a book of reproductions from the Louvre, representing the naked sinners falling and being impaled on giant thorns. Typical of religious efforts at the suppression of vice.

Attempting to read through the dream on one level—in this writing I am rerunning the images of my life, my great expectations, and in continuous performance as beforesaid; so that I keep seeing things I have seen before, and consequently am not shocked by them, though perhaps my really Great Expectation would be to reveal some drastic early crisis involving a boy in the graveyard running up against the powerful, brutal hulk of the father who is both evil (a convict) and good (a benefactor). The reasons for my not being shocked, the crude woodcut and the idea of having seen this before, represent conventional and doctrinaire views of psychoanalysis, derived from too much reading, which tell me to expect such set pieces as the primal scene, the threat of castration, and the rest. So that I continually find what I expect to find, but academically and without emotional response. It is, in effect, as though I were covertly writing, not my life, but a novel about a life rather like mine, conforming to certain conventions of psychoanalysis.

The dream thus responds to some waking thoughts I have more and more persistently had about all this, to some such effect as the following. When you test out the method of psychoanalysis so far as you are able to do, you find it is mostly a plausible fraud. The net of association, for a responsive intelligence, is endless, and endlessly intricate; moreover, it never will reach a fundamental or anagogical reading that might simplify and make sense of all the others. You could wander around this labyrinth of puns and memories for the remainder of your life, being destroyed at last merely by old age, or hunger, and not by the Minotaur (whom you will never meet, and who perhaps does not exist).

Maybe worst of all, the direction of the enterprise, instead of turning, as hoped, back toward fiction, shows signs that it will continue indefinitely producing 'analytics,' these sometimes brilliant, sometimes surprising, unfoldings of dream or memory or poem which represent, however, one more and more suspects, a power either antithetical to the power of producing art works or one to be kept strictly subordinated to the latter.

On such discouraging reflexions as these, I again come down to the thought that this work is done, or done as far as it can ever be, or as far as I can do it now. There is no self, there is only an echoing emptiness within.

And yet the doing of it, which occupied but a month, or from the tenth of July to the tenth of August in 1963, has been at many times a great delight. It produced no results—"if you want results," I said in a poem about the garbage dump of the self—or none that can be tabulated and precised in the form of mottoes, slogans, instructions to the future; it produced no result other than itself (in that way alone, perhaps, it is artistic); it made a try, and now it falls back exhausted and in some despair. Yet this is the most beautiful summer of my life, making me think sometimes of it as the last, though I don't hope that. I hope instead to continue, though in other forms than these. And maybe, in spite of everything, I will turn out to have learned a little something.

Only now, for instance, when I have resolved to put away this work for an indefinite time, the thought comes to me that the predicaments of my most characteristic and intimate imagery strangely belong to Shakespeare too, who resolved them by magical poetry in his Last Plays. May it happen to me also one day that the statue shall move and speak, and the drowned child be found, and the unearthly music sing to me.

And I wonder: What in the world can that thought mean? Does nothing belong to the self alone?

A voice speaks as though in answer, saying only: Life is the Lost and Found.

July-August, 1963

Late in this same night, our son was born.

THE POND

THE POND

At the long meadow's end, where the road runs
High on a bank, making a kind of wall,
The rains of last October slowly built
Us up this pond some hundred yards across
And deep maybe to the height of a man's thigh
At the deepest place. It was surprising how
Slowly the water gained across the land
All autumn, no one noticing, until
We had the pond where none had been before
To any memory—most surprising in
This country where we think of contours as
Fixed on a map and named and permanent,
Where even if a stream runs dry in summer
You have the stream-bed still to go by and
The chartered name—Red Branch, and Henry's Creek,
And Anthony's Race—for reassurance, though
The reason of those names be sunken with
The men who named them so, in the natural past
Before our history began to be
Written in book or map; our history,
Or the settled story that we give the world
Out of the mouths of crones and poachers
Remembering or making up our kinship
In the overgrown swamplands of the mind;
And precious little reassurance, if
You think of it, but enough about that.
Here was, at any rate, surprisingly,
This piece of water covering the ground:

The Pond

Clear blue, and pale, and crisping up to black
Squalls when the north wind moved across its face;
The question whether it would go or stay
Never came up, and no one gave it a name—
Only the water-birds on their way south
Accepted it, and rested there at night,
Coming at dusk down the meadow on wide wings
And splashing up on beating wings at dawn.

By Christmastime the pond was frozen solid
Under a foot of snow, level and white
Across the meadow so you couldn't say
Except from memory where the water was
And where the land; and maybe no grown-up
Would have remembered, but the children did
And brought their skates, and someone's father patched
Together a plough from plank and two-by-four
That half-a-dozen kids could lean against
And clear the snow down to the glittering ice.
They skated all the darkening afternoons
Until the sun burnt level on the ice,
And built their fires all along the shore
To warm their hands and feet, and skated nights
Under the full moon or the dark; the ice
Mirrored the moon's light, or the fire's, cold.
There was a tragedy, if that is what
One calls it, the newspapers called it that:
"Pond Claims First Victim" (it still had no name),
As though a monster underneath the ice
Had been in wait to capture the little boy
Skating in darkness all alone, away
From the firelight—the others heard his cry
But he was gone before they found the place—,
Or else as though, a tribe of savages,

The Pond

We sanctified our sports with sacrifice.
At any rate, the skating didn't stop
Despite the funeral and motherly gloom
And editorials; what happened was
The pond took the boy's name of Christopher,
And this was voted properly in meeting
For a memorial and would be so
On the next map, when the next map was drawn:
Christopher Pond: if the pond should still be there.

The winter set its teeth; near Eastertide
Before the pond was free of ice all night;
And by that time the birds were coming back
Leisurely, staying a day or so before
They rose and vanished in the northward sky;
Their lonely cries across the open water
Played on the cold, sweet virginal of spring
A chaste, beginning tune carried along
With a wind out of the east. Killdeer and plover
Came and were gone; grackle, starling and flicker
Settled to stay; and the sparrowhawk would stand
In the height of noon, a stillness on beating wings,
While close over the water swallows would trace
A music nearly visible in air,
Snapping at newborn flies. Slowly the pond
Warmed into life: cocoon and bud and egg,
All winter's seed and shroud, unfolded being
In the pond named for Christopher, who drowned.
By day the birds, and then the frogs at night,
Kept up a music there, part requiem,
Part hunting-song; among the growing reeds
The water boatman worked his oar, the strider
Walked between air and water, dragonfly
Climbed to be born, and dazzled on clear wings.

The Pond

Then day by day, in the heat of June, the green
World raised itself to natural arrogance,
And the air sang with summer soon to come.

In sullen August, under the massy heat
Of the sun towering in the height, I sat
At the pond's edge, the indeterminate
Soft border of what no longer was a pond
But a swamp, a marsh, with here and there a stretch
Of open water, even that half spread
With lily pads and the rich flesh of lilies.
And elsewhere life was choking on itself
As though, in spite of all the feeding there,
Death could not keep the pace and had to let
Life curb itself: pondweed and pickerel-weed
And bladderwort, eel-grass and delicate
Sundew and milfoil, peopled thick the city
Of themselves; and dragonfly and damselfly
By hundreds darted among the clustering leaves,
Striders by hundreds skated among the stalks
Of pitcher-plant and catkin; breathless the air
Under the intense quiet whining of
All things striving to breathe; the gift of life
Turning its inward heat upon itself.
So, Christopher, I thought, this is the end
Of dedication, and of the small death
We sought to make a name and sacrifice.
The long year has turned away, and the pond
Is drying up, while its remaining life
Grasps at its own throat: the proud lilies wilt,
The milfoil withers, catkins crack and fall,
The dragonfly glitters over it all;
All that your body and your given name
Could do in accidental consecrations

The Pond

Against nature, returns to nature now,
And so, Christopher, goodbye.
                              But with these thoughts
There came a dragonfly and settled down
On a stem before my eyes, and made me think
How in nature too there is a history,
And that this winged animal of light,
Before it could delight the eye, had been
In a small way a dragon of the deep,
A killer and meat-eater on the floor
Beneath the April surface of the pond;
And that it rose and cast its kind in May
As though putting away costume and mask
In the bitter play, and taking a lighter part.
And thinking so, I saw with a new eye
How nothing given us to keep is lost
Till we are lost, and immortality
Is ours until we have no use for it
And live anonymous in nature's name
Though named in human memory and art.
Not consolation, Christopher, though rain
Fill up the pond again and keep your name
Bright as the glittering water in the spring;
Not consolation, but our acquiescence.
And I made this song for a memorial
Of yourself, boy, and the dragonfly together.